THE BRITISH SKI FEDERATION GUIDE TO BETTER SKIING

THE BRITISH SKI FEDERATION
GUIDE TO BETTER
SKIING

MARTIN BELL

JOHN HYNES

JOHN SAMUEL

JOHN SHEDDEN

Photographs by Mark Junak

Pan Books London and Sydney

Contents

Foreword

Skiing has been my life since I started the sport at the age of six on holiday with my family in the Cairngorms in Scotland. Although recreational skiers can enjoy taking up skiing at any age, one of the disadvantages of competitive skiing is that it is essential to start very early in order to excel. There are no examples of ski-racers among the world's elite who learned to ski later than nine or ten. Whether you start at three or eight makes very little difference for, as the coaches of gymnasts and figure skaters have discovered, the body's kinetic learning ability is at its greatest between the ages of about nine and thirteen.

Fortunately, I was able to benefit from a large mileage on skis at this age, after my family moved to Edinburgh when I was eight. This move was prompted by our parents' own enthusiasm for skiing, and their desire to allow my brother Graham and myself to develop our potential as ski-racers, although at that time it was no more than a vague possibility. My father had asked the RAF to post him to Edinburgh as it seemed the ideal location for a skiing family. Hillend, the largest artificial slope in Britain, is situated just outside the city, and we were able to leave a caravan at a campsite near Cairngorm during the winter months, where we would commute every weekend.

At this stage, I was gaining expertise through exposure to the two main power bases of British ski racing at that time; not only was I being coached every Thursday night at the Hillend plastic slope and every weekend with the Scottish Ski Club at Cairngorm, but I had also formed links with one of the British Alpine Clubs, institutions which are based not in Britain, but in certain Alpine resorts. At the age of eight I had won a trip to Andermatt in Switzerland with the White Hare Ski Club. It was my first time away from home without my parents, but I loved the boarding-school-like atmosphere and couldn't wait to go again. That was how I came to have my first experience of real competition, when I was entered for the British Junior Championships, aged nine. I finished well down the field, but there was no one younger placed ahead of me, in fact there was no one else that young in the race.

The next year at Andermatt, I learned a

After the disasters of 1985, Martin Bell was glad to survive the first event of the 1985–86 European season at Val d'Isère with no mishaps.

different kind of lesson, when I broke my leg. We had been told to ski at speed down a slope and then turn right at the end, but I had not been paying proper attention to the instructor, and continued straight on over a blind ridge, which turned out to be a small cliff. It taught me never to go at high speed down an unknown piste if I cannot see what is ahead.

The injury was a blessing in disguise, for that year my parents decided to send me on a summer skiing trip to catch up on the training I had missed all winter with my broken leg. The only people organizing summer race training at that time were the two big Alpine Clubs, the Kandahar and Downhill Only Ski Clubs. For the next four years I went with Kandahar for two weeks each summer to Kaprun, where the British kids were integrated into an Austrian racing camp, probably the greatest single factor in improving my skiing technique. The trouble with learning new techniques is that they do not always make you ski faster immediately, and sometimes your race performances even get slower until you have mastered the new movements. Summer skiing high up on the glaciers, where the snow lasts all year round, is ideally suited for young racers who are learning new techniques, as there is no immediate pressure of competition where they must prove themselves; any races or time trials in the summer are less important and can be used to try out new things.

By now, I had an appetite for racing, but when I applied to race on the Scottish Junior circuit I was surprised to be told that no racers under the age of twelve would be accepted. Although still eleven, I had already been placed in the top twenty in the British Junior Championships and would certainly be able to produce top placings on the Scottish circuit, given the chance. It was the first, but by no means the last, time that I was to see officials in the governing bodies of the sport adhering to the rules for the rules' sake, even though those rules had been designed with the object of helping the competitor. After weeks of heated discussion, I was accepted on to the Scottish circuit, which meant a different race at a different Scottish ski area each weekend, invaluable experience for any young competitor. Regardless of the actual level of the ski racing involved, be it on snow or on plastic, regular race experience is the only way to learn certain psychological skills, such as the ability to withstand pressure; the concentration needed to find the right balance between all-out attack and safe skiing; and the most valuable lesson – to forget about a bad race as quickly as possible and prepare for the next one. In Scotland I learned how to win, but I had yet to learn how to lose.

When I was twelve I suffered from the culture shock that hits all young racers from non-Alpine countries when they first compete internationally and see how tough the competition really is. The occasion was the Donald Duck race in Norway, which, in spite of the fun-sounding name, is in fact an unofficial Scandinavian under-14s Championship. I finished about halfway down the field, over ten seconds behind the winner. Even though I won the British Junior Championship the next year, and was selected for the British Junior Team, the relative ease of this success was put into perspective by another

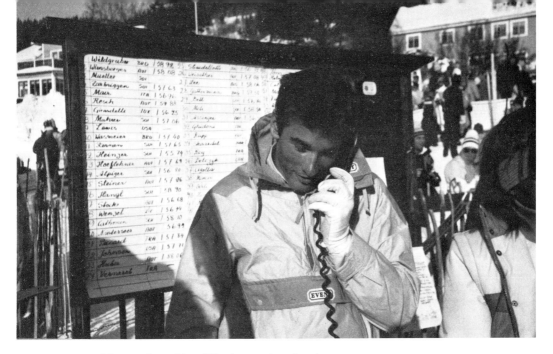

A celebratory call home after taking fifth place at Are, Sweden.

international under-14s event. This time it was the Ovomaltine Grand Prix in Switzerland, and my results were not much better. A year later, when I raced in the European Junior Championships, the time differences between me and the winners, Austrian prodigies Christian Orlainsky and Erwin Resch, could be measured not in seconds but in tens of seconds.

I had reached the nadir of the culture shock's first stage: the revelation that the best in the world are light years ahead of you and the emotional depression that goes with that knowledge. In the second stage, you no longer allow yourself to be emotionally affected by your setbacks but systematically set about working on the factors which separate you from the world's best. And the third stage? Either a breakthrough followed by eventual success, or the objective acceptance that you

do not have the talent or experience to succeed.

My progress into the second stage had already been initiated by the trainer of the British Junior Team, Peter Lorenz from Innsbruck. He emphasised the importance of fitness, not just the occasional run, but a planned long-term programme, starting with long-distance running and cycling in the summer to build up a basic endurance, followed by ever-increasing weight training, sprints and interval training in the autumn, to improve power, quickness and short-term stamina, while still keeping the endurance at an acceptable level by occasional distance work. Flexibility and suppleness should be worked on daily. For the first time ever I was doing regular condition training, or as much as was possible in the early mornings before school. I was working hard at school for my final 'highers', after which I would have the chance to change to a new academic direction. It was Peter Lorenz who suggested that I try the entrance exam for the Austrian *Gymnasium* for ski-racers; in order to compete against better racers than myself, I also had to train with better racers.

At Stams I became a truly full-time racer; I had never previously had the opportunity to ski regularly through the autumn months, or do three hours' fitness training and sports daily. I put on ten kilos as I gained strength, but one activity that was totally new to me required co-ordination rather than power: gymnastics were incorporated into the programme to increase our awareness of the position of our bodies at all times, and our ability to learn new movements quickly.

Going to school with mainly Austrian racers, I gained insight into some of the drawbacks inherent in the Austrian system, which are exactly the opposite to our own problems. In Austria, there are far too many racers competing for too few places on the various teams. Although the national A, B and C teams consist of about thirty racers, the pressure is intense and starts at an early age; if a racer has not made it on to his regional team by the age of fourteen, he is written off and there is little incentive for him to continue. Even the top racers are not secure in their position. Any newcomer to the Austrian World Cup Squad is given no chance to adjust to the tighter competition and, in the case of downhill, the more demanding courses; he must prove himself with an excellent result within his first two or three races or be removed to make way for

another newcomer, as the maximum quota for each nation is ten.

In contrast, racers in Britain who show promise at fourteen can reasonably expect to progress via the regional and junior teams into the British Ski Team without too much effort.

The base, that is the number of talented youngsters, is too small in Britain whereas it is too large in Austria. Those in Britain who advocate the 'pyramid theory' should bear in mind the pressures on the racers at the top of the pyramid should its base become too broad. The ideal situation lies somewhere between the two extremes of Britain and Austria.

My schoolmates caused me to look upon my British background in a new light. Previously I had considered myself unfortunate to have been brought up in such a backwater, in skiing terms, but now I was continually being told by the Austrians how lucky I was; I could compete in any races I wanted to, World Cups included, and could patiently learn my trade with no initial pressure to succeed. And so it was; at the age of sixteen I became British champion, competed in five World Cup races, and was even taken on a fully paid summer trip to New Zealand and Australia, stopping at Hawaii on the way home. It was too good to last, and when calamity struck, it was from a totally unexpected source. Falling down a badly covered trench in the newly-built boarding house at Stams, I tore two ligaments in my left knee, causing me to miss the entire season, including the World Championships. Surprisingly, the injury only served to strengthen my resolve to work hard at rehabilitation after my knee operation.

Britain's best: Konrad Bartelski (left) and Martin Bell support the Schools Abroad national plastic slopes final at Gloucester.

Martin Bell's sixth at the Morzine World Cup downhill in February 1986 was his breakthrough into regular top ten placings.

Watching Konrad Bartelski achieve a second place in a World Cup encouraged me even more; I knew that if he could do it, then I could do it, as I had already placed ahead of him in a downhill in New Zealand the previous summer.

When I finally got back on skis the next spring, I was keener than ever, and even went skiing on my own to build up my strength. I made a promising start to the next season, my first on the World Cup downhill circuit, but then I dislocated an elbow in the nets at Val d'Isère and had to miss much of the season. I damaged my

right knee in a downhill at Mt. Hutt, in New Zealand, and could not start autumn training until October.

The 1984 Olympic season started badly. In the first race, my brother Graham fell and injured his ankle, and in the second race I hit a rock halfway down the course, ripping a hole in my ski. To make matters worse my knee was swollen after I had tweaked it jumping off a cornice while powder skiing. Ski racing has taught me to expect only the unexpected; a disaster can appear when everything seems to be running to plan, and Lady Luck can strike down a Pirmin Zurbriggen or a Peter Mueller just when they seem to be at their most invincible. But it can work the other way as well. When we arrived at our third venue, Val Gardena, we found to our delight that the course was shortened, smooth and slow due to fresh snow, which would put the minimum of stress on our injured knee and ankle. Moreover, the course speeded up during the race, enabling me to place 14th and score my first World Cup points. The same phenomenon occurred at the Olympics; on race day, I had a touch of flu and felt miserable. But somehow my misery prevented me from dwelling on the importance of the occasion, and I skied a relaxed race to place 18th, my second best result of the season after Val Gardena.

1985 started out fairly well for me with a top thirty placing in the first race at Val Gardena, but at the second race, Kitzbühel, I crashed in every training run and lost a ski in the race. I was not injured, but I never really regained my rhythm all season and could not match my 1984 results. Graham, meantime, suffered a knee injury which eventually required an operation to keep him in racing.

Going into the 1985/86 season, I was down to my last psychological reserves. The previous winter had left me severely doubting whether I possessed the ability within me to succeed, and what kept me going was not so much a belief in myself as a stubborn desire to keep plugging away. However, the pre-season training went well, and although I kept waiting for something to go unexpectedly wrong, nothing did. In the early part of the season, I skied some good races, but more importantly I had no disastrous ones, which meant I could keep my rhythm and confidence. When I finally made the breakthrough to achieving regular top ten placings, it came as a pleasant surprise but not as a shock to me, for as I had learnt, the good racer expects only the unexpected. This was proved once again in the last race of the season, at Whistler, where after my best ever training performances and an excellent intermediate time, I crashed, something I had never done before in 36 previous World Cup downhills. It is just this unpredictability which makes ski racing so fascinating, both for the competitor and the spectator.

AUBREY FIELDER

Introduction

Aubrey Fielder is Secretary General of the British Ski Federation.

When you say 'skiing', people don't usually think of Britain. They think of mountainous countries like Switzerland, Austria and France, of powder snow and sparkling sunshine, of famous racers such as Tony Sailer, Jean-Claude Killy, Franz Klammer and Ingemar Stenmark. Few are aware of the major contribution that Britain has made to the development of the sport.

There has always been a great British mountaineering tradition. Edward Whymper was the first to conquer the Matterhorn, Alfred Mummery the Grepon – indeed it is a tradition continued today by men like Chris Bonnington, Joe Brown and Doug Scott. It was not so suprising therefore that British mountaineers such as Cecil Slingsby were among the first to take to skis in the Alps in 1880.

In fact skiing has been used as a way of getting about on snow for thousands of years. Archaeological remains found in Scandinavia, including a preserved wooden ski, and a rock painting, are thought to date from 2500 BC. But it was only a hundred years ago that skiing came to be regarded as a sport.

It was an Englishman, Mr Knocker, who introduced skiing to Meiringen in 1890, Gerald Fox who introduced skiing to Grindelwald, and the Richardson brothers who formed the first English Ski Club at Davos in 1903, a matter of weeks before the start of the Swiss Davos Ski Club and the Ski Club of Great Britain. It was also in 1903 that the Public Schools' Alpine Sports Club held a combined skating, skiing and toboggan competition at Adelboden. This continued until 1910, when cups were awarded for each event. Thus the Roberts of Kandahar race was born. On 7 January 1911 it was held on the Plaine Morte Glacier, Crans Montana, Switzerland, over a vertical drop of nearly 5,000 feet. The race was won by Cecil Hopkinson in a time of 61 minutes.

The first British Downhill Championship took place ten years later at Wengen on 5 January 1921, but it was not until nine years later that the British initiative to run downhills was followed by the Alpine nations, first the Austrians and Americans

British pioneers in the Roberts of Kandahar downhill, 1927.

in 1929, the Swiss in 1930, the Germans in 1933 and the Norwegians in 1940.

Britain's contribution to modern slalom was also considerable. Originally slalom was a style race, but the slalom as we know it today was invented by Arnold Lunn in Muerren, Switzerland, in 1922. It was also at his suggestion that the first modern slalom race held in Austria on 31 March 1928 was combined with the downhill – the downhill finish place dictating the start number for the slalom. It became known as the Arlberg–Kandahar, and is now the oldest downhill slalom event in the world. Indeed it was this event which played a significant part in securing recognition for downhill and slalom racing. At the 1930 St Moritz Congress of the Fédération Internationale de Ski, Great Britain's proposal that downhill races and modern slalom be recognized was carried unanimously. Not only did Congress accept the British proposal, but they invited Great Britain to organize the first World Championship in slalom and downhill racing in Muerren from 19–22 February 1931 – a task undertaken by the Ski Club of Great Britain and carried out with distinction.

The Ski Club of Great Britain continued to look after British interests until 1964 when it handed over to the National Ski Federation of Great Britain. This was renamed the British Ski Federation in 1981.

The British Ski Federation is the governing body of British skiing and is responsible for the training, selection and participation of British skiers on the international competitive circuit in Alpine, Nordic and Freestyle events. Only skiers who are entered by the British Ski Federation can take part in international competitions organized by the FIS.

In every skiing nation there are both ski instructors and coaches. These play different roles and you can use both to your advantage. As a visitor to ski resorts you will meet ski instructors. They have been specifically trained to work with learners – most often 'foreign' skiers visiting for one or two weeks. Ski coaches are trained to look after skiers over longer periods, perhaps for many years on a developing programme leading towards high levels of excellence within the sport. Coaches are qualified by, and answerable to, the governing body of the sport.

England, Scotland, Wales and Ulster have their own governing bodies of the sport at national level and these together with the Combined Services Winter Sports Association, the British Alpine Racing Ski Clubs, the Ski Club of Great Britain and the British Association of Ski Instructors form the British Ski Federation.

Britain continues to make a significant contribution to skiing today as more and more British skiers travel to the Alps. They not only provide income for the tourist industries of Alpine countries, but among their numbers increasingly throw up good competition racers. With the advent of package travel, ski holidays, which at one time were considered to be the preserve of the rich, are now available to everyone. Currently it is estimated that 600,000 British skiers travel abroad every year, 150,000 of them state school children.

Of course British skiers can enjoy the sport without going abroad. Scotland offers very good facilities, comparable to many found in the Alps. In the Cairngorms between five and seven thousand people may ski each weekend. Glencoe, Glenshee and Lecht are other major centres.

Television coverage has focused British attention on the thrills of skiing and this combined with the increasing number of dry ski slopes throughout the country has encouraged many to take up the sport. The first artificial slope was constructed by Dendix in 1961 as a demonstration model for Simpsons of Piccadilly. This was followed by the first outdoor slope at Pontins in Torquay in 1963, which is still working.

Today, there are more than 100 artificial slopes in Great Britain, the longest of which (400m) is at Hillend in Edinburgh. Gloucester annually stages the Schools Abroad All England Ski Championships. Such is the popularity and efficiency of these slopes that young racers whose early ski skills were learnt on the artificial slope are now entering British teams.

Young British skiers are encouraged through various state-aided schemes, whereby school children are given courses of instruction as part of their curriculum. Such schemes provide valuable instruction to the beginner but most important they broaden the base from which young racers of the future will emerge. Hopefully they will produce skiers to follow in the steps of Martin Bell, our most successful male skier for many years, and Konrad Bartelski, who achieved a magnificent second place in a World Cup downhill in Val Gardena in 1982.

Every week the Federation office in London receives numerous enquiries – from those who wish to learn to ski, who aspire to become ski instructors or who want to emulate Martin Bell. So this is a book of advice and instruction from Martin himself, John Hynes, Director of Coaching of the Scottish National Ski Council, John Shedden, Director of Coaching of the English Ski Council, and the British Association of Ski Instructors. It is a distillation of all that is best in British instruction by British experts. In it you will find a mass of information to improve your skiing and ski awareness, be you beginner, intermediate or expert.

JOHN SAMUEL

What to know off the snow

*John Samuel is ski correspondent
of the* Guardian.

Where to go

Anyone who passes for a ski expert almost certainly finds the question most frequently asked – Where do I go to ski? – the hardest to answer. In Britain, certainly if you live north of Birmingham, Scotland between mid February and late April is a distinct possibility. The Highland roads are vastly improved with motorway approaches, there is a direct train to Aviemore, and snow retention techniques and shrewd exploitation of available terrain by the Cairngorm Chairlift Company have made it possible to accommodate up to 6,000 skiers on a busy weekend. Mondays to Fridays are notably quieter.

Snow reports in the daily British press on the four main Scottish centres, Cairngorm (Aviemore), Glencoe, Glenshee and

Making for the slopes at Crans-Montana.

Lecht are fairly reliable and can be checked via British Telecom. Costs are lower than on the Continent, from a cup of tea down to lift passes and ski school, and if you are taking the measure of the sport, with a young family or as a novice, you can get a genuine feel for skiing in the more wind-protected corries, or gullies, where snow lingers far into the spring. Moreover there is the benefit of qualified British Association of Ski Instructors tuition.

People living south of Birmingham may enjoy the Scottish experience for its homeliness, but it's still a long way to go: Inverness is nearly 600 miles (960 kilometres) north of London. If you head south instead, you can fly fairly cheaply from London to Geneva, Zurich, Munich or even Milan and Salzburg in two hours or less, and have the whole of the Alps to choose from. In mid winter there's the chance of some sun, and the higher altitude snow is much better. Little wonder, then, that Austria attracts about 50 per cent of British skiers, with France, Switzerland and Italy vying for 40 per cent of the rest. Then come Norway and the USA, which are rather more expensive, and cheaper newcomers Andorra and Spain. Bulgaria, Yugoslavia and Czechoslovakia also have major ski resorts, but only Bulgaria attracts a large number of Britons, principally school parties.

For British skiers Cairngorm is convenient, and offers a long spring season, and BASI tuition.

Val d'Isere offers longer, more varied runs.

BEGINNERS

Most beginners choose their first resort by word of mouth. One of a group – and beginners will have more fun going with friends – will have heard a thing or two and encouraged the rest. The more enterprising operators offer a free place for group bookings.

A variety of specialist magazines is available in the English-speaking countries – *Ski Survey*, *Ski*, *Skiing*, *Skier*, *Ski Special* in Britain, *Ski*, *Skiing* and *Powder* in the USA. The first issues, usually in September, concentrate on places to go and how to get there. In addition there are paperback guides, for example the *Audi Ski Guide* (Ocean Publications Ltd, 34 Buckingham Palace Road, London SW1W 0RE) and the Consumer Association's *Good Skiing Guide* (Consumer Association, 14 Buckingham Street, London WC2N 6DS).

The chief considerations will be the scope of nursery slopes and their location, the ski lift service and the distance of your hotel, chalet or apartment from the slopes. Don't be fooled by prices. It is better to go low season to a well-placed hotel in a good resort than high season to a bad hotel in a snowless resort. Christmas, half-term and Easter are peak times, when prices are highest and queues longest. Other important considerations are distance from airport to resort (some of the Italian resorts are five hours from Milan), the exchange rate and cost of incidentals, and whether you speak a little of the language. In hotels, most will want only half board – a good breakfast and evening meal. Lunch for most skiers is a snack on the mountains or in a café at the base of a run.

Many Britons opt for a package holiday for its cost-saving and convenience. Usually this includes flight or coach, accommodation, insurance and possibly lessons, skis and boots. The accommodation may be in an hotel, chalet or self-catering apartment. The operator's advance block booking enables him to offer preferential terms. It is always advisable to book with 'bonded' operators so that your pre-payments are secured in the event of financial failure.

'Package' accommodation ranges from the Palace, St Moritz, to little more than dormitory living, but, more usually in Austria and Italy, it means a comfortable bedroom with bath, and frequently a swimming pool and sauna. Half-board usually means a big breakfast and evening meal served fairly early with a good choice of wine. Many family-owned Austrian hotels will organise sleigh outings or in-house games and entertainment, and their patrons return year after year at the same period which makes things even more friendly.

'Chalet' holidays these days may not involve actual chalets. The British invented them as an inexpensive form of group holiday for the under-30s in houses of the chalet type, sharing bath and sitting rooms. Meals were served by 'chalet girls', who also acted as guides and mentors for the slopes and resort facilities. Some of the original social and age distinctions of chalet holidays have disappeared, and many small hotels now provide a similar arrangement. For the gregarious it is a good way of getting started among people with a common language and enthusiasm. There is also flexibility for differing ability groups. You don't, however, meet many French, Austrians or Italians.

At least as popular are apartment holidays, especially in modern French resorts which have imported the mini-living styles of the Riviera – some of the rooms are not much larger than caravans – to the mountains. Student groups and families find them especially convenient, and most British operators service them.

Lech in Austria is one of the most atmospheric of Alpine resorts.

INTERMEDIATE TO ADVANCED

Many of the remarks addressed to beginners apply equally to those going on their third or fifty-third ski holiday. Too many people tend to lock into one country and resort, and never sample the alternatives. Everyone skis a run much better second time than first, but there comes a point where variety enhances both technique and general enjoyment.

Resorts with longer, more varied runs ought to be considered, also those with linked areas or centres – such as Courchevel–Méribel–Les Menuires, Val d'Isère–Tignes (France); Portes du Soleil (France–Switzerland); La Mongie–Barèges (Pyrenees, France); Verbier–Haute Nendaz, Davos–Klosters, St Moritz–Corvatsch, Wengen–Grindelwald–Muerren (Switzerland); Zermatt–Cervinia (Switzerland–Italy); Super Dolomiti (Italy); Montgenèvre–Sauze d'Oulx (France–Italy); Les Arcs–La Plagne (France); Kitzbühel–St Anton, Saalbach–Hinterglemm (Austria); Aspen–Snowmass, Vail–Beaver Creek, Lake Tahoe (USA). Most if not all of these have joint ski passes, a boon to the skier who likes to put in a heavy daily mileage.

More experienced skiers will often take their own cars from Britain while another alternative is fly-drive with a 'skierised' car waiting at the arrival airport. Driving on icy roads is not for the unwary. Chains are necessary at times, and the experience of driving as if on eggshells can be dearly bought. Alpine racers reckon driving a riskier enterprise than downhill skiing. For the skilful and confident, or merely the weather lucky, there are amazingly good bargains to be had in the non-package small guest house, especially in Austria. Some knowledge of German helps.

Families with young children or babies are being catered for increasingly. In France, Flaine, La Plagne and Avoriaz have a high reputation and English is generally spoken in the nurseries. There are also night-time baby services. Austria has centres catering well for children, among them Mayrhofen – especially popular with the British – and St Anton. Wengen, Switzerland, and Madesimo, Italy, are equally child orientated.

Wherever you choose to ski, you'll need snow. Increasingly, skiers are watching snow reports in the press before choosing a destination. Tour operators may well be offering discounts to secure early bookings for European resorts.

SKIING IN THE USA

A European skiing in the USA is struck by a number of differences. US skiing lives more for the day than the night. Boy meets girl on double, triple and even quadruple lifts or in the well-regulated, disciplined queues where chatting takes precedence over European-style pushing and shoving. Queue time, in general, is short because uphill is well geared to downhill. That means a lot of skiing – for beginners and intermediates as well as advanced – on groomed slopes with surfaces of packed powder, fabulous after a new snow fall and before regiments of snow cats get to work. But you have to be up early and know your way around. Although insurance premiums may be double because of the risk of cannoning into the vice-president of a major motor company and putting him off work for three months, your lift ticket builds in the cost of evacuation from the mountain. US resorts take no responsibility if you go off limits.

Moderate, slightly nervy, once-a-year skiers find themselves whistling down US slopes with undreamed of confidence and style because of the firm, smooth surface of runs cut between the trees – the US treeline is much higher out west where the latitude is that of Sicily. The mogul fields are another world. At most US resorts a few steepish fields are deliberately left ungroomed so skiers have the privilege of 'skiing the bumps'. You can go round them, through them or over them, but unlike many European resorts, where they suddenly hit you with no alternative routes, the Americans invariably offer a bypass you can cruise comfortably and with no loss of face.

At the bottom, after a long day's ski, you have the hugger-mugger of the Base Lodge, where everyone meets for lite beer, popcorn, samosas or fishy appetisers. This is US après ski before you go back to the lodges, where they serve your evening meal, or condominiums, where they don't – unless you are part of a block with its own restaurant. Condominiums are uniquely American. They are apartments, but often multi-bedroomed and lavishly equipped with many of, or more than, the comforts of home. You throw together a meal yourself (there's always a barbecue) or go and eat out.

If you buy one of the resort guides you still have to remember that grades of runs – black for difficult, red for advanced, blue for easy, green for very easy – differ from place to place. And in every place they also differ from day to day, depending on snow conditions. A 'very easy' green run may get icy and crowded at the end of the day. A steeper, uncrowded run with two or three inches of new snow may be much easier. There are no absolute and unvarying standards.

(Left) Artificial snow, produced by guns like this one at Park City, has been one of the major skiing developments of recent years.

(Below) A typical American ski scene, with runs carved between the trees, open chair lifts and children preparing for the powdery snow, at Park City, Utah.

Clothes and equipment

To some extent the novice skier and the expert need similar equipment. Both need skis, bindings, purpose-built boots and poles. They both need jacket or anorak, trousers or salopettes (dungarees) – or alternatively a one-piece suit – thick jersey, polo neck jersey or thick shirt, maybe a vest, certainly warm underpants and, in colder weather, long johns, socks of dif-fering thicknesses, hat, waterproof and warmly lined gloves. Then there are gog-gles and sun glasses, water-resistant après ski boots and a change of clothes for evening.

The difference between novice and advanced skier then opens out. Those with their own skis require a heavy duty bag, maybe a boot bag as well for those not

The skier needs water- and snow-resistant anorak, trousers (or suit), gloves, jersey, high/polo neck shirt, long underpants (long johns), socks, not necessarily too thick but higher than the tongue of the boot. Sun glasses must be stronger than for the beach. This skier lacks a hat. The head suffers greater heat loss than any other part of the body.

wishing to stow the awkward things in a suitcase. Experienced travellers prefer just two items to handle, so a double ski bag does service for a few extra clothes and the sponge bag. Very few skiers, even experts, take two pairs of skis, but skiers do get married like everyone else, and the double bag then comes into its own. Increasingly, people on half board take a snack lunch in a back pack or bum-bag, and the incidentals like money, handkerchief, sun cream, plasters and comb are less likely to be lost if carried like this.

All told, then, skiing equipment represents a pretty hefty investment. Yet more and more are doing it. For their first two holidays most people wisely rent skis, boots and poles. The drop-out rate is decreasing, thanks to better designed equipment and improved teaching techniques, but no one wants to buy stuff they may never use again. Four weeks' skiing, not necessarily all at once, is usually enough to reach a reasonable standard and it then makes sense to stop hiring and buy. At that point you know you like the sport, won't mind spending money on it, and from your experience of hired equipment, careful reading of specialist magazines and listening to the advice of friends you will have formed some preferences.

The more expert you become the more likely you are to want to trade up into sophisticated boots with forward lean adjustment, flex or cant control, easy rear entry and customized foam inners. The same goes for skis. Expert or racing models go with advanced techniques. They are made to carve rather than skid, so there is no point in a beginner/intermediate trying to cope with them too

soon. In principle, a shorter ski has more turning ability, and a longer one is more stable. When starting, it is best to err on the short side rather than the long. A simple rule of thumb is to choose skis as long as you are tall. The compact ski, about 30 centimetres shorter than a full-length ski, is used primarily for beginners to rent, and the mid-ski, from ten to twenty centimetres shorter at around 180 to 195 centimetres, is in wide general use. Full-length skis of 205 centimetres and above give an even more stable ride than the mid, but there are all sorts of variants. Soft-flexing skis are better for powder snow, with the tips rising and floating, and are more supple in mogul, or bump, fields. A harder ski will be better for hard-pack and ice. Manufacturers market an all-round ski for most types of recreational skier up to and including the advanced. Only the expert, the racer or the ski bum on the snow for much of the season will indulge the luxury of two or three pairs of skis for different conditions.

Most skis come with bindings attached, especially those bought in sales at the beginning and end of season. There is little to choose between leading brands. European test institutes have established reliable formulae for their qualities of binding, release and elasticity – the amount of give before actual release in a fall. A mid price binding will offer perfectly good protection for skiers at moderate speeds. It is important to know what setting is suitable for your weight and standard of skiing, but most shops and hirers will set them accordingly. I will tighten up, say from six to seven on the rear binding setting, after two or three days, when I have got my ski

Modern bindings are graded by European test institutes for qualities of attachment, release and elasticity.

legs and am averaging a faster speed or going into softer snow. I will also get a friend to stand on the tail while I push forward. The rear binding should release briskly. If I am in doubt with the front binding, I bang the inside tip sharply against the snow. There ought to be noticeable give, or even a crisp release of the front binding. In general it is better to release in an emergency than to stay in.

A pole of correct length should leave the forearm parallel to the ground when the tip is buried in the ground up to its basket. You can make the same test where the snow is not suitable, or you are on hard ground, by upending the pole and holding it by the point above the basket. Poles ought to be lightly weighted to assist the rhythm and timing of your turn. The pole plant is an essential feature of ski instruction. Most poles have a strapped grip. The strap should pull away in an emergency. Sword grip poles went out of fashion because people found them too easy to lose in a soft-snow fall, by jamming into the ground or dropping from a ski lift.

Deep soft snow is not so much dangerous as irritating for goodish skiers taking a tumble. A buried pole or ski is nearly always well dug in at the earliest point in the fall. Clambering back through the soft snow is an exhausting business, particularly if you are holding others up. Skiers who master soft snow say every moment of frustration is worthwhile. That has to go for skiing in general.

Insurance

Advanced skiers seeking off-piste opportunities are advised to take an experienced guide wherever they go. The risk of avalanche or pothole is ever present. Robert Blanc, who introduced ski evolutif and other major innovations at Les Arcs, was killed on a rescue expedition. Willie Bailey, a former British international skier, was killed at Verbier. US insurance statistics suggest that more people are seriously hurt hitting a tree than by any other means. The rival statistic, however, is people cannoning into each other, going fast on faster equipment than technique or experience allows. The slowest skier always has right of way, it must be remembered. Insurance premiums in the USA have rocketed recently because of costly third-party settlements.

No skier should venture out without a special insurance policy looking after all his risks – third party, evacuation from the mountain by blood wagon or helicopter, emergency treatment abroad, cancellation of hotel booking, ambulance, special travel needs for returning home and rehabilitative treatment.

These are just a few of the things that can occur. Most operators offer insurance cover. If that is not adequate – and racing may be an extra – Douglas Cox Tyrie Ltd, Saracen's Head House, 92 Fenchurch Street, London EC3M 4EA, offer a specialist service.

Insurance is a must for all skiers. The young Martin Bell shows even the best can fall.

How to get the best from ten days on the snow

For most of us who live far from the mountains, a week or two is usually as much skiing as we can look forward to in any one winter. Indeed anticipating the holiday ahead is often a great source of pleasure in itself. This pleasure and the success of your holiday can be enhanced considerably if you put your mind to it.

It all comes down to preparation. The more work you put into preparing yourself for skiing the greater will be your satisfaction and enjoyment. You can prepare yourself for skiing both before you leave home and during your stay in the ski resort.

FITNESS

Getting fit to ski is much wiser than skiing to get fit. Skiing is a dangerous activity for people not prepared to take it seriously. That applies as much to children and students as it does to adults who take no regular physical exercise. I found on my first ski holidays that even medium-paced bowling, swimming and tennis in summer and weekly soccer in winter were inadequate for the special demands of skiing. But what is an adequate exercise programme for men and women of all shapes, sizes and ages with little time for recreational sport and many other responsibilities?

Does a beginner, intermediate or advanced skier prepare on the same basis? Answer: you can have a programme which supplies most needs and does not take up much time. It is also a good exercise programme for those who may have to miss their annual ski holiday but want a general tone-up.

Skiing is deeply demanding of mental and physical resources. People with things on their mind do not ski well. Tense, over-tired muscles cause accidents. Skiers often don't know how tired they are, and falling may be the escape route of a body which has had enough, guided by a mind in automatic drive. The following exercises are especially valuable because they are aimed at the prime needs – strength, muscular endurance, agility, balance, co-ordination, flexibility and cardio-respiratory endurance. In the end it adds up to an increased enjoyment of the sport.

These exercises are best started a month before the holiday and then performed daily. Anyone with a known heart condition ought to check with a doctor before starting on them. No one should go into the full programme immediately.

Each exercise should progress gradually to the maximum number of repetitions. You're bound to feel some stiffness at first, especially in the stomach regions, but each day you should be able to reach the previous day's level and then go on. At last you begin to understand why and how a Marc Girardelli, Billy Johnson or Martin Bell will set himself a goal. Each day you will have something to aim at and find pleasure in something accomplished.

The British Alpine team in fitness training at Val d'Isère.

EXERCISES

	maximum number of repetitions
1 Standing, legs slightly apart, circle the arms, forwards then backwards.	× 10
2 Single sprint start jump. Arms braced on the floor, legs straight out behind. One leg and then the other jumped up under the body, then back.	× 10 each leg
3 Step up on to a chair or stool, bringing the feet together, then step down on to the floor the other side. Then a step back, bringing feet together again, then a step down to the original position.	10 each
4 Same as No 2 but with both legs brought up under the chest into the squat position. Hips should be two inches (5cm) from the floor when legs are straight.	× 15
5 Lying on the back, sit up, curling the back as you do.	× 10

	maximum number of repetitions
6 Star jumps. Starting in the squat position, leap off the floor throwing arms and legs out wide in a star shape, finishing in a squat which is not too deep.	× 5
7 Cycling. Shoulders on the floor, hands on hips, legs straight up in the air, rotate legs as in cycling.	× 20
8 Jack-knife. Lying on the back, lift both legs to 45 degrees, sit up and touch the toes, knees bent towards the chest.	× 10
9 Balancing. Standing on a stair balanced on toes and balls of feet, drop the heels until the calves tighten. Then return to the original position.	× 10
10 Burpees. Combination of No 4 (double sprint start) and No 6 (star jump).	× 5

The Park City Ski School's Mountain Experience Class explores areas not usually skied by the public.

SKI CLUBS

If you think of skiing simply as a holiday activity, to be practised *only* during your visit to the snow, then this fitness programme will have given you a good start to your holiday. On the other hand, if you find skiing becoming more than this – a sport which you would like to follow throughout the year – then join a ski club. Relating your holiday to a regular skiing programme will give much more meaning to what you do on the snow. You might even decide to take up competitive skiing.

Even if you do not want to race, joining a club will put you in touch with other skiers. The shared enthusiasm of skiing will increase the pleasure of your holiday and you may even end up travelling with other members of the club.

A further benefit of joining a club is that you may have access to a coach. In this case your ten days on the snow will become simply an exhilarating extension to your coaching programme which will ensure that you get the best from yourself during your holiday.

DRY SKI SLOPES

There are now dry ski slopes within easy access of most towns. Most have clubs attached to them, some with ski schools and instructors. Whether you are being introduced to skiing for the first time, or brushing up before you go skiing again, you will find it well worth your while to visit a dry ski slope. Dry slopes provide an ideal medium for getting fit for your holiday – combine your exercise sessions with dry slope skiing once a week and you will be physically very well prepared.

If you go along to your local dry ski slope for the first time expecting to find a mini alp you will be very disappointed. Some dry centres are neither as clean nor as tidy as they could be, but most are now very pleasant places to visit, especially when they are busy with other skiers all enjoying themselves.

Dry slopes are not snow. This may seem too obvious to be worth mentioning, but I must, because so many skiers, used to the sparkling snow of mid winter in the fairytale setting of an Alpine village are disappointed when they first see the bristles of the matting and find everyone wearing jeans or old clothes in case they fall over.

The sounds and colours are not the same and the surface is less slippery than snow. This is both a blessing and a nuisance. It is annoying to skiers used only to perfect piste, because it is not very forgiving. On the other hand, because it demands more accurate movements, it helps you to improve your technique quite quickly. If you consider the dry slope to be simply another variety of skiing surface,

It isn't snow . . . but plastic slopes help to improve technique quite quickly.

like powder snow, soft damp snow, good piste, heavy wet snow, wind crust, ice, slush or frozen corn snow, then you will develop an accuracy and versatility in your skiing which will really enhance your holiday sport.

PREPARATION IN THE SKI RESORT

If you have prepared yourself well, all you need to do now is to keep yourself and your equipment in tiptop condition for the whole of your holiday. To ski your best every day, aim to start each morning in good condition, feeling fit, alert and ready to go. This will be easy if you take the following hints, and check them off one by one each day. Do not be worried or too serious about this, just build them into your daily routine and your time on the snow will be as enjoyable as it can be.

However fit you are when you arrive, do not overdo it for the first few days. Skiing all day will take its toll of your energy stores. Make sure of the following:

a Walk and stretch a little before breakfast.

b Eat a good breakfast and follow with a complete, balanced diet through the day. Eat plenty of fruit and/or vitamin C.

c At altitude and because the air is dry it is relatively easy to become dehydrated which will in turn effect your co-ordination, visual perception and general health. Drink plenty of fluids which contain water.

d Change your underwear as often as possible, and in any event change into *clean* washed socks every day. Perspiration causes salt crystals to lodge in the fibres of your socks and they can rub, causing sore or blistered feet. Nothing is guaranteed to spoil your skiing more than sore feet.

e Always dry your clothes thoroughly each night. If your ski boots are damp and cold, take the inner boots out, and dry them in your bedroom. Remember your *feet* are the only contact you have with your skis – look after them!

f Look after your skis as well. After all, your preparation and anticipation will have been to no avail if your skis will not do what you ask of them. Whether you buy or hire, your skis should be in excellent condition when you arrive in the resort. So each evening, before you settle in for the night, give your skis and sticks a 'once over' check.

Are they all intact?

Sticks Handles firm? Shaft still straight after the fall this afternoon? Are the baskets in place?

Boots Are all the buckles intact? No stitching undone? Inners dry?

Skis Are the soles clean and free from gouges? Are the edges smooth and intact? Are the bindings clean and with all the screws in place? Are the adjustments the same as when you started?

If you find any problems with your equipment, try to sort it out before dinner – the ski shops are usually open until early evening. Always be ready to start promptly the next morning.

Stay tuned: broken skis and limbs can follow if skis and bindings are neglected.

TUNING YOUR SKIS

Skis are very sophisticated precision machines. That is why they cost so much more than the barrel staves and one piece wooden skis that they have replaced in modern times. To get the best out of your skiing ability you need to get the best out of your skis. This means restoring them to their precision design whenever they wear significantly. Competitive skiers restore and tune their skis every day – sometimes twice a day, between runs of a slalom. For the average holiday skier, however, every three or four days will keep your skis performing at their optimum.

You can easily do this yourself if you take the necessary tools. Alternatively, you can ask the ski shop to do it for you. Either way it is an inconvenience, but when you have experienced the effect of regularly tuned and serviced skis you will gladly put up with the bother.

You need:
* A straight-edged scraper
* P. Tex candle or similar strips
* A small file
* A sheet of emery cloth
* A packet of 'universal' wax and a travelling iron to apply it.

If possible, practise tuning first on an old pair of skis.
1 Find somewhere to place your ski sole upwards.
2 Check that the sole is flat (with the straight edge) and there are no big scratches. If there are, fill them in with melted polythene strip. The ski shop where you bought it will tell/show you how to use it.
3 Check the edges for burrs. These are likely to be under your feet, inside edges.
4 If there are, use your file, firmly but carefully, to return the edges to a smooth, square cross section.
5 Remove the file burrs with the emery paper.
6 Dull the edges back from the tip and tail of the ski (about 6 in (15 cm) and 2 in (5 cm) on the inside edges and 7 in (18 cm) and 3 in (8 cm) on the outside edges). This is not critical and serves to allow you to use the instep of your feet effectively without the tip or tail grabbing or hooking.
7 Finally, clean the soles with a clean rag and then melt wax on to them in a smooth thin layer, and when it is dry and hard, scrape it off again. Throw the scraped-off wax away!
8 If you want to tune your skis to perfection you might like to learn how to bevel the soles/edges. This is done by filing the sole across either side at an angle of about 1° so that the edges are higher than the middle of the sole, *when the ski is flat on the snow.* The benefit of this is considerable, but it requires a good eye and a steady hand.

Bevelling reduces the tendency of a ski to grab or hook – without having to dull or detune the edges. It makes it easier to 'change edge' during a swinging series of turns, so aiding the initiation of the turns. Most of all, however, bevelling lifts the edges a little off the snow and so enhances the gliding/sliding ability of the ski. Skis that slide easily are easier to steer and of course, if you are a racer – they run just that little bit faster.

If you decide to bevel your skis, remem-

ber: do not overdo it. 1° each way is suf-
ficient – any more will probably spoil the
grip characteristics of your skis. (1° is
about the thickness of this page.)

Martin Bell taking good care of his skis.

SKI INSTRUCTION

If you are an intermediate or advanced skier you may feel you are past joining the local ski school. If you are travelling with your ski club you may be fortunate to have your own qualified coach to guide you and this is of course ideal if your overriding wish is to improve your skiing skill. If you are not so fortunate, or if you are on holiday alone, then remember never to ski alone. If joining the ski school does not appeal to you, then consider hiring a ski teacher for private lessons. Do this on your second day, after you have found your ski legs and early enough to benefit from his or her local knowledge as well as the technical content of the lessons.

Then all you have to do is get to the slope, and enjoy yourself!

For the gregarious beginner, joining the local ski school may be the best way to pick up technical tips.

JOHN HYNES AND JOHN SHEDDEN

Part One: Basic techniques

John Hynes is the Scottish National Ski Council's Director of Coaching.

Techniques for level terrain

In order to get to the 'level terrain' where you're going to start skiing, you'll probably have to walk from a carpark or bus stop. You owe it to your fellow skiers to carry your skis and sticks in as safe and considerate a manner as possible. The safest way to carry skis is over one shoulder, with the tips pointing forward and down. The skis should be held together by a ski tie or by the ski brakes incorporated in the ski bindings. The point of balance is usually with the toe piece roughly just behind the neck, sticks carried in the other hand, pointing down.

Having arrived at the level terrain at the bottom of the nursery slope, you will probably notice a build up of snow on the sole of your ski boot. This will have to be removed before you step into the bindings. If the snow is relatively soft, it can usually be knocked off by tapping the side

The sociable way to carry your skis: tips forward and down, point of balance with toe-piece just behind the neck.

Snow sticking to the bottom of the boot must be knocked off, otherwise the binding's release mechanism may be affected.

43

of the boot with a ski stick. If the snow is harder, you have to scrape it off on the edge of a ski. As a last resort get someone to help remove the snow, otherwise it could impede the release mechanism of your ski binding.

Now that your boot is free of snow, you can step into your bindings. Make sure your skis are lying flat and parallel on the snow. Carefully place the toe of the boot in the toepice of the binding, line up the heel of the boot with the heel piece of the binding and press down firmly. Assuming that your bindings have been correctly adjusted (and this should be done by an expert in the ski hire shop) you will not have to stamp. If you do have to stamp to get into your bindings, there is something wrong with the adjustments or you have *not* cleared the sole of your boot properly.

Once you have both skis on, the next thing to learn is how to hold the ski sticks correctly. Slip your whole hand through the strap from below so that the inside of the strap lies against your wrist. Enfold both sides of the strap between thumb and forefinger and close your hand firmly around the strap and stick handle.

You are now ready to try moving with skis on. At first you may feel as if you have acquired feet that are about two metres long. You will have to get used to handling these ungainly objects, so some ski familiarization exercises are called for. Start with an easy one. Lift the tail of one ski in the air, leaving the tip on the ground. Make sure your ski sticks are firmly planted on either side to support you. Do this with alternate skis, then try to lift the whole ski off the ground. This gives you an idea of the weight of your equip-

Stepping into the binding: toe first,

Grasping the stick: slip the hand through the loop from below.

ment. Other exercises include sliding your skis backwards and forwards alternately on the spot, and rocking your skis gently from side to side to get the feel of the edges.

Now you are ready to go for a walk. A good maxim is to start with small steps which are less tiring and easier to control than large ones. Slide the skis across the snow. They will slide very easily but it helps if you angle your sticks backwards so that you can use your arms to push as well. To change direction you will have to

then hard down with the heel so that the rear binding clicks shut over the heel welt.

(Below) You may feel as if you've acquired feet two metres long . . . Lift the tail first, leaving the tip on the ground, then the whole ski.

angle the tips of your skis one at a time, being careful not to cross your skis at the back. Having practised this, a useful aid and indeed a test is to set a line of ski sticks or slalom poles and try to 'wander' through them.

Start with small steps, then set a line of sticks or poles and try to 'wander' through them.

The nursery slopes. No top skier has started later than nine or ten.

SIDESTEPPING

By now you should be ready to try climbing uphill on your skis. Obviously you can't walk straight uphill. The lack of friction or traction between your skis and the slippery surface you are standing on combined with gravity dictate otherwise. There are two ways to climb when wearing skis. The easiest way is to sidestep. If you were to make a snowball and let it run down the hill, it would take the steepest or most direct line. This is called the 'fall-line'. Turn your skis until they are at right angles to the fall-line, and tilt them on to their uphill edges. It is essential at this stage to bend your ankles and press your knees over your toes. This will enable you to rock your skis on to their edges and hold them there while sidestepping.

Hold the lower ski on its uphill or inside edge and step slightly forward and sideways with your uphill ski. The same maxim of small steps applies. Set the ski on its uphill or outside edge and hold it there while bringing the lower ski alongside. Repeat this procedure as long as necessary to attain the desired height. Keep your sticks out of the way.

Keeping stable . . . It is essential to bend your ankles and press your knees over your toes.

HERRINGBONE

The other and more strenuous, albeit more efficient, way to climb uphill is called 'herringbone'. Face uphill and form a wide V with your skis by placing the tips well apart. Press your knees straight forward so that your skis come on to their inside edges. You will feel somewhat knock-kneed. Place your ski sticks behind you with the palms of your hands on top of the handles for support. Then walk uphill using opposite sticks for support (left leg, right stick) making sure you hold the ski on its inside edge. The track you leave in the snow gives this method its name. Small steps are the order of the day again. Once you have attained the desired height, bring your skis across the fall-line and rest on your uphill edges.

Before we go on to basic schussing, let's have a look at some of the problems you may have encountered, and the possible solutions.

1   When walking or sliding on flat terrain make sure to bend your legs at the knees and hips to lift the tails of the skis off the snow. Try to maintain an alert athletic posture.

2   When sidestepping, because the position of the bindings is on the rear half of the skis (the toepiece is roughly in the middle of the ski) the front half of the ski feels heavy and the tendency is to leave the tips behind. Make sure you lift the tip well off the snow. (Curl your toes upwards.)

3   When using the herringbone method of climbing, make sure the tail of the moving ski clears the stationary one, or you will get some nasty scratches on the top surface.

4   Getting up after a fall. The technique of falling (which happens to the best of us) is covered by John Shedden later in the book. At this stage, let us assume that you have had a gentle touchdown and you would like to get up again. Get your skis

Getting up from a fall . . . Draw the feet up under the body . . .

Herringbone help . . . Make sure you lift the tail to clear the stationary ski.

across the fall-line below you, and draw your feet up underneath your body by bending your legs. You can then use either your hand to push up or your ski sticks as a lever.

Learning to use gravity

SCHUSSING

Gravity is what makes it difficult for us to climb uphill, but conversely makes it easy for us to ski downhill. In fact it causes us to do so. What this means is that unlike runners or other athletes who require muscle power to generate propulsion, skiers get their motive power from gravity. Muscle power is used to control movements. It was muscle power which enabled you to climb uphill; gravity will now take you back down again. As long as you are on a slope gravity will keep pulling you downhill. Since you have not yet learned the techniques of controlling your descent, make sure before you start that you have a counter slope or a flat runout area to bring you to halt. Ideally you are looking for a slope with reasonably soft snow (certainly not icy) with a texture which aids edge control, particularly when stepping around.

In order to try your first basic schuss, you have to face downhill. The easiest way is to use your ski sticks as aids. Plant them approximately a metre downhill from your skis, one opposite your feet and the other halfway between your toes and the tips of your skis. Place the palms of your hands on top of the handles and straighten your arms. Ideally, your sticks have now become extensions to your arms. Supporting yourself on your arms, move your skis round in small steps, being careful not to cross your tips or tails until you are facing straight downhill between your sticks. If

Preparing for the first schuss. Use your ski sticks to help you.

you wish you can use this stepping technique as a means of turning round to face in the opposite direction.

Maiden descent . . . Carry your hands forward and out, and literally let yourself go.

You are now ready to try your maiden descent. 'Walk' your sticks back uphill one at a time until you are standing upright. Ideally your legs should be roughly hip width apart (open stance), which will give you a broad base to stand on and improve lateral stability, with equal weight on both feet. Flex your ankles, knees and hips, and stand in a relaxed free posture. Carry your hands forward and out from your body (arms akimbo) to aid balance and let yourself go, literally. When viewed from the side all the 'Ski Joints' are flexed and the back is slightly rounded. If a line were to be drawn through the body, it could be

seen that the body weight is carried directly over the balls of the feet.

Remember, you are sliding downhill, so ideally your imaginary line should be at right angles to the line of the slope. When you are standing still you were balanced statically. When you are moving downhill, you need to be balanced dynamically, in order to adapt to the speed of movement (however fast or slow) and any undulations in the terrain. Dynamic balance therefore can be roughly defined as balance whilst in motion, a pre-requisite for all skiers. This is the most fundamental part of your ski technique. In *The PGA*

Dynamic balance . . . weight over the balls of the feet. You should always be at right angles to the slope.

European Tour Guide to Better Golf, in this series, Tony Jacklin says, 'Nothing is more important for a start than a proper grip, and yet only one in five amateurs I see acknowledges this need.' So it is in skiing with your basic stance. It is the key to your future success in mastering the skill of ski-ing. A good posture will aid dynamic balance and greatly shorten your learning time and subsequently increase your enjoyment of the sport.

When you have had several goes at this basic schussing, try to develop some flexibility by bending down to touch your boots as you approach the runout area.

USING A BABY TOW

Avoiding a hang-up. Take your time: the operator will look after you.

Many ski resorts and artificial slopes have 'baby tows' specifically serving nursery areas, with gentle runouts or counter-slopes. Should you decide to use one of these the first thing to do is to tell the operator that you have never been on one before. He will help you overcome your initial uncertainty. There is a technique involved, however. When the people in front of you have gone, step carefully across to the mounting point. Take your time, the operator will look after you. Stand with your skis facing uphill and watch for the hanger coming over your inside shoulder. Transfer both sticks to your outside hand. If the hanger is a T-bar the operator will probably hand it to you. The cord in the hanger drum will start to extend until it is at full length. There will be a slight jerk as you take off, so be ready for it. Once moving, the tow has replaced gravity, so stand on your skis as normal and literally ski uphill. A word of warning. Lift operators in this position often get ski sticks up their noses, so keep the points down and facing backwards or forwards as shown in the photos.

In some areas, it may be a button tow of some sort, which you may have to catch yourself. In this case, having caught it, place it between your legs, be ready for the jerk, and once it is moving, follow the same principle of skiing uphill. At the top of the tow, watch out for warning signs telling you what to do. They will either tell you simply to let go of the hanger, or feed it round the return wheel. In either case, once you have done so, move quickly to the side to avoid skiers coming up behind you or being struck by a swinging hanger.

Now that you are more or less mobile, you should practise and develop a variety of movements. For instance, you can improve your flexibility and develop your perceptual skills by getting someone to throw a glove at different angles for you to catch.

Be prepared for the jerk; then stand normally to be towed along.

Be flexible: catching a glove takes away stiffness.

SIDE SLIPPING

If when you arrive at the top of the tow the slope appears a little too steep to ski straight down, there is another way of using gravity to help you get down safely. You can sidestep downhill, or even better you can side slip. Side slipping can be defined as brushing the edges of the skis over the snow (or artificial surface). To do it, start with your skis at right angles to the fall-line on the edges, as with side-stepping. Make sure your ankles, knees and hips are flexed. Turn your upper body and face completely downhill. Plant your ski sticks on the snow behind and uphill of you. Reduce the amount of edge you are holding by gently rolling your knees outward until they are over your toes (no further), and at the same time push yourself sideways down the hill with your ski sticks. Remember to keep your upper body over your feet, and don't leave your sticks behind. You can stop anytime you want, by pressing your knees into the hill and resetting your edges. Once the side-slip has started, gravity will keep you moving. If you find you are having to push with your sticks all of the time, the chances are you are overedging. Practise varying the amount of edge set to control your speed. The less edge you set, the faster you will sideslip, and vice-versa.

If you find that you are moving forwards as well as sideways, then your weight is probably too far back, and you are allowing your skis to turn downhill. Correct this by standing in the middle of your skis, and turn your feet across the fall-line. 'Knees over your toes' is a good maxim here.

Starting the slide . . . push yourself sideways down the hill with your sticks.

If you have difficulty releasing the edges to start the slip, try pushing your lower ski downhill first (not too far) and pull the upper one behind. Make sure it stays on its upper edge, albeit less of an edge than for sidestepping. Maintain this movement, shuffling your feet at the same time until you start slipping.

You are now doing elementary side slipping and you are well on your way to becoming a skier.

Controlling motion

It is all very well to allow gravity to pull you downhill, but at this stage you could be forgiven for feeling rather like a car with no steering and no brakes. Sooner or later you are going to have to change direction, if for no other reason than to avoid an obstacle, which could be another skier. (Skiing is generally regarded as a non-contact sport, après-ski being considered the 'contact' side of the sport.)

Let us assume that you are skiing downhill in a straight schuss, and you need to change direction. Cast your mind back to when you 'wandered' through ski sticks on level terrain by angling your skis at the tip. The same principle can be applied while schussing, provided you have maintained your dynamic balance by keeping all your ski joints flexed.

Start at a level on the slope where you are happy about the speed you will attain, and as you ski downhill, transfer all of your weight to one foot and hold your skis parallel for a few metres. Since our photographs show the skier stepping to the left, I will describe those movements. When you feel ready, lift the tip of your left ski and angle it to your left. Remember the maxim of small steps still applies at this stage – you do not want to outreach yourself. Be ready to react a bit quicker now, because once you put your left ski back down on to the snow, your skis will be going in different directions.

By angling your ski like this, you have in fact turned your leg. Apart from turning it, you also have to move it sideways. Ideally your body should move across with your leg. This means that as your left ski contacts the snow, your weight will already be on that leg, which will make it easy for you to lift your right ski back alongside your left. Repeat the movement as often as necessary to attain the desired change of direction.

As you come further round the corner,

your skis will probably start to skid a little. Don't worry about this. The cure, if you can manage it, is to try to set the skis on their edges a little, as in sidestepping. It will feel rather like an angled sidestep on the move, and initially you will probably feel a trifle ungainly. Again, don't worry: this is a normal reaction.

Practise this on both sides, trying to improve your athleticism with each attempt. You will probably soon become aware that you are happier going to one side than the other. Again, this is normal. Just as you have a dominant hand by being right or left handed, so too you will have a dominant leg which you will be happier to stand on. You should however practise until you are proficient on both sides.

Changing direction. Don't worry about skidding or that you favour one side or the other – it's normal.

SNOWPLOUGH GLIDE AND BRAKE

There are other ways of controlling your motion while skiing downhill. One of the most elementary ways is by forming a 'V' with your skis by diverging the tails. The technical term for this manoeuvre is a 'snowplough', so called because of the shape the skis make.

Still using the nursery area with a run-out, lean on your sticks and face downhill as for a straight schuss. Keep the tips of your skis about six to eight centimetres apart (roughly the width of the basket on your ski stick). Step or slide the tails of your skis out until they are about a metre apart. Raise your sticks and ski down the hill in this position. It is important to maintain the snowplough formation of your skis. Keep your weight evenly distributed on both skis and your ski joints flexed as for schussing. In fact, when viewed from

Tails a metre apart

Side on, the schussing posture

the side, your posture is very similar to the posture adopted for schussing.

Practise this 'snowplough glide' several times until you feel comfortable with it. Initially you may find that your skis feel as if they have a mind of their own and want to run together. At first you will probably use leg strength to maintain the position. A simpler way is to relax and sag on to your skis. In this way your body weight will help you to hold the position.

Now it is time to start experimenting with the width of the 'plough'. Press your ski tails further apart, maintaining the tips the same distance apart as before. You can do this either by extending your legs (using leg strength) or by sagging or drop-ping your weight more between your skis. What you will notice immediately is that you will start to slow down. Your downhill speed will decrease. If you make the plough wide enough, you will stop. Prac-tise varying the width of your plough from wide to narrow to wide again. This is called 'snowplough gliding and braking'. You have now learned that the narrower the plough, the faster you will go and the wider the plough, the slower you will go downhill. You will soon learn to develop what I call the 'learning plough' where you will learn to judge just how wide to make it in order to maintain a constant speed downhill.

(Right) Vary from wide to narrow.

TRAVERSING

Another way to control your motion is to go across the hill at an angle. This is called 'traversing'. Because your skis are pointed across, you will have to place them on their edges as in sidestepping. To help you to hold the edge, flex the ski joints and press your knees into the hill, at the same time leaning slightly outwards, or away from the hill, with your upper body.

Keep your feet apart to aid balance. In this position, because of the outward lean of the upper body and the inward lean of the lower leg, you will carry more weight on the lower ski than on the upper.

Because you are crossing a slope, one foot will be higher than the other, which will mean that your upper ankle is bent more than your lower. Advance your uphill ski until both ankles are bent to the same extent. To feel comfortable, turn your hips and shoulders so that they face a direction roughly parallel with an imaginary line drawn across your ski tips. To stop, step your ski tips uphill.

Press your knees into the hill.

Practise going from side to side down the hill, varying the angle of descent until you can judge what is a comfortable speed for you. To improve edge control, practise lifting the tail of your uphill ski and hold it in the air for two seconds or so, whilst traversing.

You have now learned one of the fundamentals of skiing.

To stop, step your ski tips uphill.

Steering and turning

SNOWPLOUGH TURNS

You can now control your motion going down fairly easy or gentle slopes. But your repertoire is still somewhat limited, and obviously you would like to be able to change direction without having to step round all of the time. At your level of skiing, the easiest way of doing this is to develop the theme of snowplough gliding and braking.

When you push your heels out to go from a narrow gliding plough to a wider braking plough, you are in fact turning your legs. Because you are doing both simultaneously, and in opposite directions, one counteracts the other and this keeps you going in a straight line, albeit at a slower speed because you have set the skis more on their edges and the wider plough creates resistance to downhill travel over a wider area.

Can you imagine what would happen if you pushed out on only one leg? What would happen is that you would change direction. In other words, if you maintain your snowplough with both skis on their inside edges, you can go from side to side by turning one leg at a time. Let's look at this in a little more detail. Stay on the same gentle terrain that you have been skiing on and start skiing downhill in a gliding plough. When you feel ready, push the tail of your left ski out to help start the turn, then press your left knee forward and slightly in. You will start to turn to your right. So long as you keep doing this, you

Keep pushing on the left tail and you'll keep on turning.

will keep turning. It is important to understand what is happening here. By pushing the tail of the ski out, you are turning that leg. By pressing the knee forward and in, you are bending the leg and shortening it in comparison to the other, thus dropping more weight on to the ski. The turning characteristics of skis are described in more detail later in the book. Suffice it to say here that by applying more weight to the ski when it is on its edge, you cause the shape of the ski to become distorted which, in fact, causes the ski to turn.

To link your turn to the right with a turn to the left, stand up and re-assert your gliding plough by equally weighting both skis. Your skis will start to turn towards the fall-line again.

You can aid this by gently pushing out the tail of your right ski. When you are facing downhill once more, press your right knee forward and in and you will turn to your left. When you stand up, you are 'unweighting' the ski, which makes it easier to start turning it to the fall-line. When you sink down and press your knee forward and in, you are effectively steering the ski out of the fall-line. Therefore, the formula is, up to the fall-line, down out of the fall-line. Because you are shortening first one leg and then the other, you are transferring your weight to the turning ski each time. When turning to the right it is the left ski, and when turning to the left it is the right ski.

Your hips and upper body should stay in a calm, relaxed, quiet position. It is the legs that do the work here.

When viewed from behind, you can see that this method results in a somewhat skiddy type of turn.

Rear view . . . a skiddy type of turn.

For the faster, more aggressive skier, here is a more dynamic type of snowplough turn to try. In this one, there is no up and down movement, the turn being made purely by leg rotation. Start in a narrow wedge-shaped snowplough with both legs bent by pressing both knees forward and in. This will set the skis more on their edges. It will require more leg strength to hold this position. As you ski downhill, extend the turning leg and turn your foot at the same time. As the snow resists your

A snow plough with just the legs rotating results in a faster, more 'carved' turn.

(Left) The different leg uses for the two snowplough turns.
(Above) Turning round sticks is a test of control.

Rhythm is the business . . . women often make a better start than men.

efforts to do this, you will feel the edge bite and the ski will distort and start to turn. Transfer your weight on to the ski and steer it round the corner with your knee. Link these turns by extending first one leg, then the other, maintaining a neutral position with the hips and upper body throughout. This results in a faster, more 'carved' turn.

Whatever type of snowplough turn you have opted for, try testing your abilities and control by setting some ski sticks in the snow and skiing round them at different speeds.

Go on now to develop your ploughs to descend the hillside. Select suitable ski runs and learn to control your speed as you ski downhill, enjoying the sensation of freedom. Remember, the further round the corner you turn, the slower you will go. Try to develop rhythm as soon as possible, as this is one of the keys to better skiing.

Before we finish this chapter on snowplough techniques, it is perhaps worth observing how the difference in sex will affect how you ski. Apart from the difference in strength, women will tend to have a wider hip girdle in relation to body shape than men. Generally speaking therefore, where a man's femur (thigh bone) tends to come straight down from the hip, a woman's angles in towards the knee. What this means in skiing terms is that initially, when learning snowploughing and traversing, women will perform more efficiently than men because they will naturally be able to set the ski on a better edge. They do find it difficult to hold the edge at very high speeds because of the strength factor and also will usually have a little more difficulty in initiating side slip because they have further to roll the lower knee out to release the edge. If any couples take up skiing together, therefore, the man should not take it as a blow to his male ego if his wife or girlfriend seems to be able to ski better than he does to start with.

All of this apart, as a coach I have observed that generally speaking women tend to make better students than men simply because they do not try to compensate for lack of technique by using strength and therefore are more inclined to pay attention to the advice of their instructor.

BASIC SWING TURN

Parallel swings to the hill

The 'basic swing' will enable you to ski with more fluency and cope with more difficult terrain. Generally speaking, this turn is designed to help the less stable skier, since it works by keeping both skis in contact with the snow throughout the whole manoeuvre.

In the snowplough turn, the edges were preset for you and all you had to think about was steering with one leg at a time. In the basic swing turn, you start with the skis parallel on both upper edges and change the edges one at a time as you turn until you have completed the turn and are on the new upper edges going in the opposite direction.

Let us study this in more detail. Set off in a traverse and, when ready, rise and displace your skis into a narrow or gliding plough. Already you have changed one edge (the outside ski is now on its inside edge). Turn your skis until you are facing approximately downhill, then slightly advance the inside ski and roll the knee outwards to change the edge on that ski.

This will enable you to draw it in parallel to your outside ski, all the time maintaining contact with the snow. You should then be able to finish the turn with a swing to the hill. The point to remember is that as you turn to the fall-line, you must transfer your weight to the outside in order to be able to draw the inside ski parallel.

STEM SWING

Skiers with better stability can try a stem swing instead of a basic swing, the difference being that in the basic swing both skis are displaced in a plough to get to the fall-line and in a stem swing only one ski is displaced.

From a traverse, stand on the lower ski, lift the tail of the upper ski and displace it in a 'stem' position. When you place it back on to the snow, make certain it is on

The stem turns displaces only one ski

its inside edge. Now you must bring your inside ski parallel. To do this, transfer all of your weight to the stemmed ski and lift the inside ski in at the same time changing the edge. If you have a little difficulty in doing this part of the turn, you can use the ski stick as an aid to closing the ski. Plant it just before lifting the ski in. Because of the necessity to stand first on one foot and then the other while moving, this turn should only be tried by the more stable or experienced skier.

Learning to read the mountain

Experiment with your repertoire now. Practise your manoeuvres on easy terrain to improve or refine them. Combine your techniques in sequence, using different techniques on different parts of the mountain. Your basic swing will enable you to cope with easy terrain. As the terrain gets steeper or perhaps a little bumpy, then your stem swing might be more useful. Learn to read the mountain. On wide open pistes you will have no real problems. If you find yourself approaching a gully or a bottleneck you should anticipate finding not only more people in your way and less room to turn, but because more people have been turning there, you can expect to find bumps or 'moguls'. If you arrive at a steep part of the mountain which you have to negotiate in order to get to an easier part, use it as an opportunity to practise your side slipping or skidding.

In the Alps when skiing forest trails, be careful as you approach a corner. The chances are that someone may be lying on the piste just around it. This isn't as silly as it sounds. Because they cannot see around the corner, most people will tense up a bit. This very tension is liable to lead to error and cause them to fall. Look well ahead when you ski. Watch for drifts of deeper snow or patches of ice and be ready to adapt your balance. Anticipate that a drift will slow you down and move your weight back a little to accommodate this. Conversely, for ice, anticipate your skis trying to get out from underneath you and get your weight right over your feet.

Don't be too proud simply to skid over a patch of ice with your feet apart until you can get to a piece of snow on which you can turn. In short, develop a relationship between your ability as a skier, the techniques at your disposal and the terrain to which you are applying those techniques. Familiarize yourself with the Skier's Courtesy Code of the FIS (International Ski Federation). They are as follows:

1 Consideration for others. All skiers must behave in a way that will not endanger or injure others.

2 Control of speed and manner of skiing. Every skier must adapt his or her speed and method of skiing to the terrain and prevailing weather conditions.

3 Choice of course. The skier must select his or her course in such a way that he or she does not endanger those in front of him or her. Skiers approaching each other on opposite traverses should pass to the left. Keep left is the rule.

4 Overtaking. A skier can overtake either on the right or the left but he or she must always allow the overtaken skier to have plenty of room for movement.

5 Joining or crossing a piste. A skier who wants to join or traverse a piste must first look up and down the piste to make sure he or she can do so safely. The same applies every time a skier stops.

6 Stopping on a piste. A skier must avoid wherever possible stopping in narrow sections of a piste or on bends. A skier who falls should make the way clear again as quickly as possible.

7 Climbing. When climbing or walking on a piste, always keep to the edge. In poor visibility, leave the piste altogether.

8 Obey every sign. All skiers should

observe piste markings and warning signs and at all times co-operate with lift staff and the Ski Patrol.

9 Accidents. In the event of an accident, every skier is obliged to stop and offer assistance.

10 Identification. Anyone involved in or witnessing an accident must give details of his or her identity if asked to do so.

Learn to understand the international coding for grading ski runs in terms of difficulty.

Green = very easy. Blue = easy. Red = intermediate. Black = difficult.

You should also be familiar with the international ski run warning signs.

In other words, get to know the mountain. Also, be well aware of the risks of being in a mountain environment. Here are some points to consider:

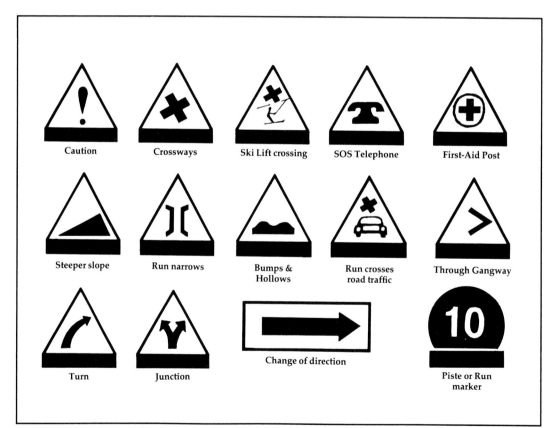

International ski signs

1 *Temperature* For every 300 metre rise in altitude there is a 2°C drop in temperature in overcast conditions (cloud acts as a blanket) and in dry, clear conditions the drop may be 3°–4°C. In Britain the difference between valleys and mountain summits could be 10°C (15°–20°F). In Alpine areas the difference may be much greater.

2 *Wind* Mountains can be very exposed to wind and the strength on summits may be several times as strong as in valleys. Wind and temperature act together on the body to produce a cooling effect known as wind chill. The more strenuous the effort, the greater the cooling effect. With moderate energy output, a temperature of 10°C (50°F) and a wind speed of 15 mph (24 kph) cause cooling of an unprotected body equivalent to that of still air at −13°C (9°F), a reduction of 23°C (41°F).

3 *Weather signs and forecasting* Although meteorology is a demanding science, it is possible to become moderately proficient in forecasting local weather changes by:
i study of a few texts and interpretation of weather maps in the national press;
ii careful observation of cloud forms and other natural phenomena.

For further information see:
The Weather Guide (Forsdyke),
Mountain Weather for Climbers (Unwin).

4 *Cold weather clothing – basic principles* Wear thermal or woollen underclothing, several thin over-layers rather than one or two thick ones, and a windproof outer shell. Pay particular attention to head covering and hands.

5 *Hypothermia or exposure* On mountains this usually occurs in cold, windy and often wet weather in individuals who are hungry and fatigued.

Symptoms: Shivering, pallor, complaints of coldness, listlessness, failure to understand instructions, violent and abusive language, failure of vision and collapse into coma.
Treatment: Prevent further heat loss. Proceed to shelter and rewarm. Feed with glucose and hot, sweet drinks. *Never give alcohol.*
Prevention: Ensure adequate clothing. Ensure adequate food intake. Descend to shelter in severe conditions.

6 *Frostbite* This occurs in similar conditions to those which may induce hypothermia. Frostbite may be either:
i superficial ('frostnip'),
ii deep.
i is much more common in skiing and is rapidly reversible by gentle warming and protection of affected extremities such as nose, fingers, ears, etc.
Symptoms: White patches on cheeks, etc. Flesh cold and soft and victim can feel little or nothing in affected area.
Prevention: Adequate clothing. Adequate food intake. Avoid constrictions. Alertness to risk.

7 *Sunburn* A common injury to skiers, particularly during periods when sun is warm and snow cover extensive.
Prevention: Use suitable suncream (protection factor 10–15), and lip salve to protect lips.

8 *Snowblindness* Another common injury, particularly when conditions are bright and snow cover extensive; may also occur in cloudy or overcast conditions when victim is operating without adequate protection.
Symptoms: Watering and inflammation of eyes, headaches, inability to tolerate bright light, blindness with great pain (usually temporary).

Prevention: Use of good quality glasses or goggles (seaside sunglasses won't be strong enough).

9 *Acute mountain sickness* Usually only severe above 3,000 metres but milder symptoms affect many at lower Alpine altitudes.

Symptoms: Severe lassitude, frontal headaches, nausea, vomiting, loss of appetite and sleeplessness.

Treatment: Descend to lower altitude and rest. If symptoms persist seek medical advice.

Prevention: Avoid over-exertion initially at altitude. Take frequent rests until acclimatized after a few days.

With forethought and care, none of those problems should occur. It would be foolhardy, however, not to be aware of them. It would be a great pity to spoil your skiing holiday for the lack of a few simple precautions.

All skiers must behave in a way that will not endanger or injure others.

JOHN SHEDDEN AND JOHN HYNES

Part Two: Advanced techniques

John Shedden is the English National Ski Council's Director of Coaching.

Ski technique is never an end in itself. When you have mastered your own body movements and those of your skis in one particular technique, you should practise them on easy slopes. In this way you will be able to attend to the movements themselves rather than the other problems posed by more difficult terrain.

After you have developed a small degree of 'automation' in your techniques, you should practise on, and seek to adapt to, a variety of slopes with different gradients and textures.

Develop variety in your movements and versatility of techniques: this is the key to greater skill and skiing expertise.

Ideally we would all like to flow easily down the hill in complete harmony with our environment. On steep terrain, however, some skiers build up too much speed because they don't come far enough round the corner. In other words, they don't finish the turn. This often results in a loss of control and usually a loss of fluency. You could say if you like that they are 'overflowing'. Defensive skiers on the other hand are inclined to come too far round the corner to keep the speed down. In other words, they overturn in order to resist the build up of speed. This again results in a loss of fluency as they try to regain speed after each turn. You could say in their case that they are over-resisting.

There is obviously a happy medium and to achieve it we must strike a balance between flow and resistance. Ideally as you ski down the hill you should be constantly assessing the terrain. What you perceive will affect how you feel emotionally, which in turn will affect the technique you employ to cope with that particular piece of terrain.

Expert skiing . . . the search for the happy medium.

Feeling at home on the hillside.

Skiing parallel

There are two approaches to learning to ski parallel. One is to attempt to do something you cannot (yet) do – to try to make parallel turns. The second and more realistic approach is simply to ski, learn to read the terrain, feel at home on the hillside and comfortable with a little more speed and then *use your speed* to cause small changes to what you can do already.

This second approach involves the development of basic building blocks, but once established these building blocks will enable you simply to change how you ski, by adding speed and emphasizing your movements. The building blocks are:
*   Selection of terrain.
*   Good dynamic balance with the ability to steer the skis.
*   Feeling for the snow.
*   Sense of rhythm.
*   Feeling for flow.

This stage of your skiing career is the vital link between being a beginner – learning the basic building blocks – and being an advanced skier who can use these principles to ski or to flow down the mountain in harmony with the terrain. Because movements and body shapes are learned, initially at slow speeds, your greatest problem to overcome is that of using fixed or static body position to flow with. Practise good posture with sound basic movements, and then increase your speed on carefully selected terrain. Now you are ready to use your speed.

Being successful, in sport, in work or in life, often depends on what your goals are. How successful you are as a skier will also depend upon the nature and the speci-ficity of the goals you set yourself. It is a goal of most beginners to learn how to make parallel turns – but is this a sensible goal?

Viewed from the perspective of a beginner the parallel turn is singularly attractive. It is what experts appear to do all the time and it is what ski instructors demonstrate so beautifully. It is written about by journalists and illustrated in books. It, in a word, is singular.

Beginners can do only one thing at a time – that is what makes them beginners. Therefore it is reasonable to try to do ski techniques one at a time. For ski instructors trying to explain to their classes what they are doing when they demonstrate, one single turn is as much information as can be handled by the group. In books, what is described or depicted is abstract, therefore one turn is as good as another, and therefore one turn is usually all that is shown in order to illustrate the salient points of the technique.

The parallel turn is thus a very understandable and marketable manoeuvre. The only problem with all this is that it doesn't exist in the real world – at least not in the real world of skilful skiers.

If you set yourself the goal of making parallel turns you are not likely to be very satisfied when you achieve your goal.

A much more realistic and useful goal to set yourself is that of skiing parallel. Here the emphasis is on skiing rather than parallel and in practice it is a statement of probabilities rather than certainties. By this I mean that to be a skilful skier – an expert – you should be prepared to accept that not *all* your movements will be as you would ideally wish them to be.

Some movements, made while in motion down the slope from your initial vantage point, will require modifications, responses made to the terrain, snow conditions, or other skiers who were not even there when you set off. If you set off with the aim of making each turn discrete, isolated from those before and after, and text-book perfect, then your descent is likely to be a series of perfectly executed turns, but jerky, stilted and less than satisfactory in response to circumstances encountered en route.

You should attend to where you are going. Shift the emphasis from parallel to skiing and the parallels will take care of themselves – most of the time.

THE WHOLE GAME

Learning to ski is somewhat like learning to play soccer. Skiing mostly parallel from start to finish of a ski run is like playing a match, scoring a goal and winning. A parallel turn in this context is much like making a pass, trapping a high ball, dribbling, moving into an empty space to draw the defenders or taking a corner kick.

To improve your game you should keep a balance between playing the *whole* game and working on the *parts* by taking them out of the game, setting and practising them in order to improve quality, consistency, and a level of habitual automation.

Next time you go to a ski centre take a close look at the game that the better skiers are playing. As an example, watch a slalom or a giant slalom race to see skiers tested to their limit in their whole game. Alternatively, watch the off-piste skiers as you ascend in the cable car. What are the main characteristics of the way they play their game?
* The run begins and ends in control. This implies good judgement and pre-selection of appropriate terrain.

* Not too steep – not too shallow.
* There are no traverses – except to choose a new line of descent or to the café for a Glühwein.
* The descent is a sequence of deflections, each smooth and round and linked with a clear and probably powerful rhythm.
* The skis will probably be parallel for most of the time but no attempt is made to keep them parallel *all* the time. The skilful skier times his movements so that although his skis may be quite close together, they are always working independently and each step from foot to foot occurs as an integral part of the rhythmical pattern of movements.
* No two turns are ever the same. As speed, terrain, snow conditions and the way a skier feels change so each turn – each deflection of flow – is adapted to embrace these changes. Any single descent will be a continuous adaptation to an ever-changing environment, but within which there are some relatively constant elements.

84

PRACTICE

In order to develop your skiing parallel, these are the elements or the parts of the game that you should practise.

1 Ski down smooth and easy slopes, with good flow, making rhythmically linked skidded turns. Initially it does not matter how these turns are initiated (i.e. what their names are), it only matters that there is a good, clear rhythm and you can feel when you are skidding.

2 Imagine a channel, a corridor, to the edges of which you must ski – say about two metres wide. Take your turning pattern out to this width in most turns.

4 On artificial slopes you can use the seams in the mats as a guide and use either one mat or two mat widths as your target corridor.

5 As you begin, use a plough but with your skis *almost* parallel and *wider* than hip width apart. As you get under way, allow the inner ski to swing or float closer to the outer ski, but do not actively bring it towards the outer ski.

You may find that you tend to stand on both feet and move your hips or upper body too much. In this case try pedalling. As you press against the outer ski to

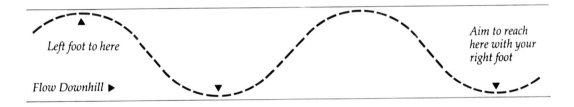

Left foot to here

Flow Downhill ▶

Aim to reach here with your right foot

When you have established your rhythm, try to go faster but keep going out to the full width of your corridor. In this way you will *feel* how you actively seek more flow and then resist as you skid, in alternative phases. You will find this easy if you keep your upper body and head quite still, but use vigorous extensions and flexions of your legs. And remember . . . you are a biped. Press or step from foot to foot.

3 Imagine your flow to be down the centre of the channel, but use your feet, especially the instep of your outer foot, to steer your ski from edge to edge of this imaginary channel.

deform it into reverse camber, press against the big toe; remember, do so with a slight leg extension and at the same time flex the other leg and lift the tip of the inner ski slightly. Confine the extension to your ankle and knee – keeping your hips slightly flexed at *all* times. After several hours of practice at this game you should be able to finish each descent skiing parallel.

There are two particular reasons why it is important to establish a sound rhythm. Fistly the rhythm of your movements will take you on to the next part of the pattern even if you make an error in any one turn. If you make turns in isolation any error will cause a complete breakdown of your movements, and a considerable loss of control.

The second reason is however the more important. Whenever you make a sequence of turns, the first turn is always different from the second, third and all the others. When you make your first turn you are often travelling slowly and always changing linear into angular momentum. It is of course hard to skid – a prerequisite of all parallel turns – when you don't have enough momentum, but much more significant are the forces required to create turning motion from linear or straight line motion.

For this reason, you will always find the first turn not only different but more difficult than all the others. Bear this in mind whenever you practise a single movement in isolation.

These two reasons for making rhythmically linked turns are encapsulated in the Austrian idea of *schwingen*. The swinging action of a pendulum cannot be correctly demonstrated one phase at a time. The whole action is greater than the sum of the parts.

PRACTICE

1 *Swing to the hill*
From a steep traverse – with reasonable momentum – flex your ankles, knees and hips. Press against the ball of the lower foot and turn both legs and feet to steer the skis in a curving skid.
2 *The fan*
This refers to the fan-like pattern on the snow made by practising the swing to the hill from steeper and steeper traverses until you are skidding uphill after descending the fall-line.
3 *Controlling the radius*
This is achieved by a combination of greater skidding – by turning your skis more across your momentum – and of sensitive edging. This you do by moving your thighs forward and in towards the centre of the turning arc, while balancing against your instep.

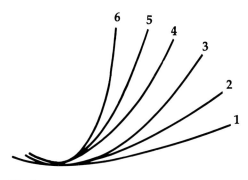

The fan.

This combination of turning and edging the ski results in an increase in pressure against that ski – initially against the shovel – which deforms it into a reverse camber arc, and this too helps to steer the turn.

4 *Starting the skid*
If you have any difficulty starting the skid, which you then steer around the arc, use the principle learned in the plough swing.

As you gather momentum in your approach to the skid/swing to the hill, stand tall on your heels. Now sink down forward against the ball of the lower foot. This movement means you will emphasize your momentum in relation to your skis – which turn across it.

Use both your legs – *independently*. Begin in a steep descent, and stand not only on the heels, but more specifically on the heel of the upper or inner ski of the anticipated turn. As you move forward and down, step down against the ball of the lower or outer ski.

Now you are ready to cross the fall-line. Simply repeat the last exercise – step from one heel, down against the ball of the other foot and steer your skidding skis uphill. This time, however, before your skis turn too far uphill and you lose too much momentum, simply step against the ball of the other foot and make a swing to the hill in the opposite direction.

As you continue these swings you will realize that the fall-line is not now significant. What matters is your sense of direction of flow and it is your flow line that you cross when you step against the new outer ski to begin the next turn.

This exercise makes it very easy to turn your skis in a parallel mode. You must however keep them at least hip width apart and then you will find it easy to move from instep to instep – to use the design of the skis and to prevent your hips from moving out over the skis which would reduce the effectiveness of your 'bicycle-lean-in' angle of the leg.

SKIDDING

Skidding occurs whenever you turn your skis, more or less 'edged', across your momentum – provided that you have enough momentum to keep going, or tend to keep going in the direction of your momentum, as the resistance increases at your skis. This concept of skidding is the single most important factor for controlling both speed and direction for all skiers.

If you think of skidding as something you can do either basically or with great refinement, and either symmetrically or asymmetrically in relation to your neutral posture, then all ski techniques which involve skidding become very simple to understand and to perform.

If you ski in a straight line, gather momentum, and then displace both skis, more or less edged, at an angle to your momentum, your skis will skid. As the resistance to your flow builds up, you do of course need to adjust your posture, especially the angle or inclination of your legs, in order to remain in good balance.

Skidding in this way – with symmetrical displacement – is called ploughing, and with exactly the same ingredients performed asymmetrically it is called parallel skidding.

Just as you can steer your plough, so you can steer all aspects of skidding. The basic ingredients are very simple and it will help you to develop your skiing if you can perform these basic ingredients well. As a beginner, you used basic skidding or ploughing as a means of slowing down or stopping. As you learn to read the terrain, and move at higher speeds, you should use your skidding to *deflect* rather than oppose your momentum.

This is most easily achieved by making rhythmical turns. In the early stages, make one deflection (turn) at a time, but as your movements and your balance responses become more automatic, more habitual, then reduce the time and distance between deflections (turns) until you are deflecting your flow, rhythmically quite close to your flow line, which will tend to be close to the fall-line of the hillside.

PRACTICE

Establish momentum, and then by displacing one ski at an angle, edged slightly, balance against it and skid. This will deflect your motion which you should now channel or funnel into a narrow pattern of rhythmically linked deflections. As your flow line and the fall-line of the hill come closer together, so it will be easier to skid providing you do not make any harsh movements.

PLOUGHING FOR SPEED

If you think of snow ploughing as a beginner's technique only for slowing down then you will have difficulties in developing your skiing. On the other hand if you modify your plough so that it deflects your motion, *without* slowing you down very much, you will soon emerge from your chrysalis and ski fluently and skilfully.

Narrow your plough. Keep your feet wider than hip width apart, but open the tips of the skis so that they are only slightly ploughed. Now ski the funnel again, this time *feeling* for the deflection of your motion as you push out against the outer ski.

PRACTICE

On easy, smooth terrain, repeat the funnel many times. That is, with a narrow plough angle, tips wide apart, funnel your turns closer to the fall-line until you are making *rhythmically* linked deflections.

Ploughing with both legs may mean that the inner leg ski of your turns opposes your changes of direction. In this case you need to steer the inner ski as well as the outer, to skid your skis asymmetrically. Isolate this movement by practising the plough swing.

PLOUGH SWING

This is an exercise which teaches you to
i   turn your inner leg and ski
and
ii balance against asymmetrically skidding skis.
*   Plough with reasonable momentum. Stand up quite tall and feel that both skis are skidding (symmetrically).
*   Begin to bend forward, flexing at the hips, knees and ankles, taking your hands well down with straightish arms.
*   As your legs bend, bend the inner leg more than the outer leg, i.e. bend your left leg if turning left.
*   As you bend the inner leg, turn it so that you move the ski-tips *apart*.
*   During these movements your outer ski has been supporting your weight and resisting your momentum and remained skidding.
*   As you put the other ski on the snow again, both skis are now at an angle to your momentum and will skid – and because they are both facing the same direction you will tend to go forward (in the direction your skis point) as well as sideways (in the direction of your momentum).

As you establish your plough, stand tall on your *heels*. As you bend forward, move down against the *balls of your feet*. This action ensures that your momentum is maintained while the skis begin to resist it.

Use the shape of your skis to help you turn, skid and steer them. The design of a ski is basically very simple. The 'sidecut' means that the ski is narrower at the waist (middle) and even at the heels than at the shovel. Thus when you *move* pressure forward against the shovel of the ski, when it is edged or tilted at a slight angle to the snow, this wider part of the ski tends to grip more than the middle; and because the ski is also more flexible at the front, its forebody bends into an arc – into reverse camber. This gripping, curved part of the ski, combined with the effect of your momentum, being transferred to the ski at your feet – behind the shovel – means that the ski will begin both to skid and to turn – steered along a curved path by the shape of the reverse camber of the ski *and* the pressure from the snow (resistance) pushing it off the line of your momentum.

If you are too anxious to make the skis turn too soon, or you are travelling too slowly, you will tend to stand on or put your weight on your outer ski. If this happens, your hips will move over that ski, and your balancing and steering ability will be seriously hindered. Instead, use the plough to establish the lean in angle of your leg before you use it to support you *as* you turn.

When you turn or corner while running, skating or cycling you must lean your legs or your bike over *into* the bend. So it is with skiing! Thus because the legs are leaning in when you are ploughing, the removal (by bending and turning) of the inner leg will ensure that you turn as long as you have enough momentum – enough speed – and you keep pressing down and out *against* your support foot. That is, the outer foot of your turn.

Use the shape of your skis to help you turn, skid and steer them.

VARIATIONS ON THE PARALLEL THEME

When you make one parallel turn you will notice that the most difficult part is the point at which you change your edges. This is not because changing edges is difficult, but because balancing while you do so is. At least, it is difficult if you are making a single turn. On the other hand if you have followed my advice and learned to make a sequence of linked turns – to keep turning – then the balancing in motion is easier and the moment of edge change is not so noticeable.

If you find it is still a problem practise this part in isolation, then put it back into the whole game.

You need to time the edge change in harmony with your total leg movements. In its simplest form, you can achieve a very satisfactory edge change during a small hop, or light spring.

As you finish a swing to the hill you will be crouching – pressing down through the soles of your feet (mostly one foot – the outer foot). Feel this posture as a ready-to-spring posture and so bring up off your toes with a good ankle and knee extension. As your skis become light you can turn them at a slight angle to your momentum and as you land you will do so against the new edges.

You can spring as vigorously as you wish – this will enhance your balance – or you can simply extend fluently and unweight your skis.

To aid the timing and the symmetry of your movements use a double pole plant. As you sink in the skid phase of the swing uphill, bring the points of your ski poles forward. Jab both poles in simultaneously and press down on them as you spring upwards. Use your ski poles to help, but never use them instead of, your legs.

Once you have mastered the coordination of skidding – sinking/pressure, jab, spring, land gently and skid again – you can use your ski poles alternately to trigger each turn in sequence.

When you can feel your flow along your chosen route, and control your rhythm with deflections from side to side, from foot to foot, you will notice that because you emphasize the steering action of your skis rather more than any other single aspect, you are able to steer them over undulating terrain.

The skidding turn.

PRACTICE

Seek out moguled or undulating slopes and practise bending and stretching your legs as you cross the high and low points of the terrain. Make long arcs, balancing against the outer ski and as that ski rises on bumps, bend your leg and as it crosses hollows, extend your leg to follow the contours and keep your ski under turning pressure. If you attend to flexing and extending to follow the contours, you will soon be able to steer your skis irrespective of whether your legs are bending or straightening.

This means that you are now ready to ski moguls successfully simply by choosing a pathway which is appropriate to your anxiety level, and to ski in soft or deep snow simply by being sensitive to the feedback you get from your skis as they turn you, and by standing a little more evenly against both feet throughout the whole descent.

As you approach your goal of skiing parallel, you will realize that athletic movement from foot to foot and sensitive adaptation to the terrain are the most important elements of successful descents, and skiing parallel is something that comes very easily if you accept a high probability of success rather than 100 per cent perfection at every step.

DYNAMIC BALANCE

If on a shallow, smooth slope, you let gravity do most of the work, and most especially if you copy only the single movements of your ski instructor, one at a time, then you may become an intermediate skier with quite stylish but relatively fixed body positions. You may even find yourself thinking and talking about skiing 'positions'. For example 'snowplough positions' or 'traverse positions'. Such ideas will inhibit your skiing in the future, because as the terrain gets steeper, the surfaces more varied and your speed faster, fixed body positions will neither allow you to balance nor enable you to control your skis efficiently and effectively.

Your body uses a different balance mode when it is moving and in motion from when it is stationary. You can see the problem. On shallow, smooth slopes, with gravity supplying the power, your body's balance reflexes may think that you are not moving. You might adopt a static, or responsive, balance. You may find yourself standing too upright, with one or both legs quite stiff and your weight carried through your heels – all perfectly normal when you are standing still, but very counterproductive when you are in motion. The solution is to develop good dynamic balance, also called anticipatory balance.

By following the advice given in the earlier part of this book you will have built strong foundations for good dynamic balance. As the terrain becomes steeper and your skis slide more quickly, you must maintain a positive approach to balancing in motion. You must try to be athletic in your movements. Use your legs and arms, despite the awkward equipment, as you would if you were running or skipping and most especially as if you were running and dodging along curving pathways. In this way your normal reflexes and athletic movements learned off skis will enable your body to balance while in motion.

There are several factors which distinguish the dynamic balancing mode from the static balancing mode. You can practise these while skiing on easy terrain.

PRACTICE

The intermediate skier has to rid himself of fixed body positions.
Advanced to expert skiers are agile and flexible.

Select a smooth slope of easy gradient and make a series of continuously linked turns. It does not matter what sort of turns you make as long as they are linked with a reasonable rhythm.

1   To be agile and athletic, move lightly, using good ankle flexions *and* extension to spring from foot to foot.
*   Develop independent leg action.
2   Lower your whole body by flexing at

ankles, knees and hips. This ready-for-action posture will have your back inclining with your shins.
* Flex a little.
3 Move off your heels and use the balls of your feet, and even your toes, when you press on the front of your skis and when you spring from foot to foot. When you are balancing in motion
* Stand on the whole length of your feet.
4 As your speed increases, or if you are anxious for any reason, your arms will tend to bend and your elbows may be pulled backwards.

To reduce your anxiety and to improve your balance, straighten your arms during every turn and move them away to the sides and slightly forward of the vertical.

Many beginners make the mistake of holding their arms and hands too far forward. The ideal placing of the arms is in relation to the vertical and gravity rather than the body. In other words, the arms should simply hang from the shoulders and yet also be alert and ready for action.
* Move your arms slightly forward and sideways as you flex and hold your sticks so that they diverge behind you.
5 To aid your balance your sensory apparatus – your eyes, ears and touch receptors – need to work within a simple frame of reference. Try to keep your head quiet and feel for your movement flow.
* Keep your eyeline horizontal.
6 As an intermediate skier you will be familiar with the expression 'keeping your weight against the outside ski'. You may even have been told to 'lean out' in order

to achieve this. The value of these expressions is important but the precise meaning may not be as you first thought.

As a skier making turns you are an object moving along curving pathways and must obey the laws of motion that all such objects in motion adhere to. Thus like a rider on a bicycle or motor bike, like an ice-skater or a 200 metre sprint runner, you must lean in as you round the turn. To be precise, your legs must lean inwards and your trunk should remain more or less upright – to facilitate your balance in case your feet (and skis) should unexpectedly slip out sideways. You should use the strongest part of your foot, your instep, to support you, as the centrifugal effect of turning can cause your inertia to exert a force of several times your normal body-weight along your leg during the turns.

In each turn you will therefore feel yourself resisting your motion through your outer leg, which should be leaning inwards towards the central axis of the turn.
* Lean the outer leg – inwards.

The development and enhancement of sound dynamic balance will mean that you no longer think in terms of skiing *positions*. You will now be aware of the *act* of snow-ploughing, aware of the movements that you must make, continuously, to keep the skis doing what you intend them to do. Your body shape will now soften and become looser. You will cease to hold fixed body positions and begin to move in harmony with your motion and with the terrain.

STYLE

The characteristics of a skilled skier, embodied in good style, are whole body movements which range from extreme flexion to complete extension and yet appear to the observer to be quiet and fluent. On smooth, shallow slopes you may have thought that a quiet style was due to holding fixed body positions, but as you move on to steeper slopes, become more athletic and gain more speed you realize that quiet is nothing to with feeling quiet. On the contrary it arises from very dynamic movements, but movements which keep the body mass on a smooth and fluent line of motion.

In this context, motion refers to the path of your centre of mass as it flows down the mountainside. Movement refers to the changing relationships of your body parts – your legs, arms, trunk etc. On the ski slopes, muscles generate your movements while gravity powers your motion. Centre of mass is the theoretical point at which the mass of the body is considered to be concentrated. The shape and distribution of your body mass determine this point. It has no actual placement in the body as a physical spot, but nevertheless it acts as a

Using speed to maximum effect . . . US Olympic downhill champion, Bill Johnson, at Aspen, Colorado.

simple reference concept which enables you to understand what is happening when you ski, and what you can do to improve your skiing ability.

As an intermediate skier you may have learned by traditional teaching methods which were very 'body position' or movement orientated. Sequential and serial movement patterns are easily demonstrated and easily copied by pupils eager to learn the latest movements, the latest techniques. The result of this preoccupation with movement patterns alone is usually stilted, mechanical and far from graceful.

If there is a single element in those skiers who are said to be naturals it is their feeling for, and their awareness of, their motion, and perhaps more than this, a willingness and intention to control and direct their motion. It has often been said that the technical movements of skiing are easy – the difficult part is doing them while sliding down a tilted, bumpy white and featureless, very slippery world – and staying sort of upright at the same time.

Trying to direct your motion is a combination of balancing and feeling for the effects of your movements. To make the step across the plateau which separates the intermediate leisure skier from the advanced and expert skier you must explore the relationships between your movements and your motion. Develop these relationships in harmony with the terrain and learn to use your speed.

LEARNING TO USE SPEED

Good style and quiet, efficient movements are always the hallmark of skilled performers; but in skiing there are some very important differences in the movements and motion of beginners and experts which you must appreciate if you are to develop your own style to match that of your teacher.

In general terms, beginners move quite slowly on shallow slopes, which are usually quite smooth, while experts can ski in control on more varied, steeper slopes at higher speeds.

Your first steps on skis were almost certainly made on smooth, completely flat terrain and your movements and your motion were therefore powered entirely by your own muscles. It is generally agreed that cross-country ski racing, which is practised essentially on level terrain, is the most physically, i.e. aerobically, demanding of all sports.

As your ability improved your muscle power was replaced by gravity to power your motion, and your muscles were required to control the movements of your body and thus your skis.

So you can see that skiing on shallow slopes can have the advantage of reducing the amount of physical work you have to do, and will also reduce anxiety.

Smooth, shallow slopes have the advantage that your balance will not be disturbed very much. Therefore you can give into gravity and slide downhill without having to change your posture very much. Without really trying you can adopt the style of the better skiers.

CHOOSING TERRAIN

At this stage of development in your skiing your choice of ski slopes will have as great an influence as any other single factor. It is important to recognize the difference between developing your ability and simply performing, using what you can already do in order to descend the mountain.

You will be tempted to get as many black runs under your belt, in a day, as you can. This would be one measure of your current ability. On the other hand, with a view to developing your technique you should select easier slopes, smooth red runs, and even blue runs if they are wide gentle pistes. On such slopes you will feel safe and able to explore new movements without inhibitions caused by anxiety or the need to rush or modify parts of your movements to cope with terrain problems.

The best skiers in the world, the World Cup racers, test their abilities on steep and icy slopes. But out of the racing season

Pirmin Zurbriggen, world downhill champion, at Aspen. Even the top skiers experiment on less challenging terrain.

Top woman . . . Erika Hess, Switzerland's 1982 world champion, suffered a lapse of form when coaches tried to alter her style for the hinged gates. She has reverted to a rounder, smoother flow line and in 1986 shared top World Cup slalom position with Austria's Roswitha Steiner.

they develop their skill by experimenting with new movements and consolidating the basic movements on quite shallow and easy terrain. After all if they cannot do it perfectly under ideal conditions, there is no possibility of doing well under difficult conditions. This principle applies to all.

On the slopes you select to practise on, there will be features such as bumps which will aid your unweighting or initiate a side slip. There will be small ridges or banks which will support you if the snow is very hard or icy, and other features which can be used to assist individual techniques. By all means use these features if it is convenient, but do not go out of your way to make isolated movements to suit the terrain, rather seek to establish sound rhythms in your movements so that your motion, along predetermined pathways or curving lines, is as constant and as regular as possible.

THE FLOW LINE

As your speed increases so too does your momentum. In your days as a beginner, skiing at very slow speeds, the fall-line of the slope had an overwhelming effect on your movements. Now the importance of the fall-line remains but your own flow line becomes increasingly significant as your speed, and hence your momentum, increases.

As you become sensitive to your motion down the hillside, so you will be aware of the fluency of your motion, your tendency to flow down the hillside. Your flow is the amount, and most importantly, the direction of your momentum.

Consider how a small trickle of water runs downhill – down the fall-line initially. However, as the stream grows into a torrent, gathering momentum, it will tend to swing wide on the bends and even flow uphill sometimes when it runs against a counterslope. It is gravity which powers the initial movement of water, but the speed of the torrent will add its effect to gravity and shape the course of the stream according to its momentum. So it will be with your skiing. As you build up speed, the direction of your flow – your momentum at any given moment – is as important as the fall-line of the hill.

Recognizing and then channelling your flow is the essence of advanced skiing. Moving your skis so that you resist your flow is how you control both your speed and direction of travel. In other words, how you deflect your momentum and thus keep it manageable, both technically and emotionally.

At the simplest level you simply choose a very shallow slope on which your momentum will never build up beyond manageable proportions. At its most sophisticated you may learn to use your skis so sensitively, and with such strength, accuracy and refined balance that you are able to carve along perfect arcs.

LINKING YOUR TURNS

At this level you should never be static on your skis. On steep terrain particularly, try to link your turns, with one flowing into another. To achieve this, the steering action which finishes one turn is the preparation to start the next. Your legs should always be either bending or stretching and constantly turning.

your upper body should virtually face the fall-line, as you angulate from the hips. Bring your lower ski stick forward and plant it as a trigger to start the next turn.

Because of your speed and the steepness of the terrain, the unweighting action need not be so pronounced. Take the turning pressure off the outside ski by 'uncoiling'

On steep terrain the steering action to finish a turn is severe. The lower stick is a trigger for the next turn.

Because of the steepness of the terrain and the build up of momentum, the steering action required to finish a turn is quite extreme. Remember, momentum is trying to force you downhill and you are trying to resist. Almost all of your weight and turning pressure should be on the lower or outside ski as you hold it on its edge. Although your legs are rotating,

so to speak and lifting the ski just off the snow. It is now about to become the inside ski of the next turn. Your momentum should transfer easily across to the other ski, the outer ski of the new turn. It will cause that ski to be weighted and help the new turn to start. Having changed the pressure, change the edges by rolling your thighs across. This will cause a strong

Lifting the outside ski helps the uncoiling. The inward lean is strong from the knees down.

inward lean of the lower legs, that is, from the knees down, and enable you to steer the skis around the corner in a smooth arc. If you can think in terms of forming arcs in the snow as you ski, with the arcs all linking smoothly together, then you are on the way to achieving the balance between flow and resistance.

A tip here is to make use of the whole length of the skis. In other words, instead of carrying your weight just on the balls of your feet, carry it along the whole length of your feet. This will bring the tails of your skis into play and enable you to hold an edge along the length of the whole skis and prevent the tails breaking away.

Smooth linked arcs are assisted by carrying weight from toe to heel, not just the balls of the feet. Tails will not then break away.

103

SKIING MOGULS

One of the problems of linking turns in this manner is that as more and more skiers do it on the same piste, eventually bumps or 'moguls' will form. They can cause problems for the less experienced skier. The advanced skier can use them to his or her advantage. When you watch a car travelling over rough ground, the body appears relatively still while the wheels move up and down furiously on their shock absorbers. When skiing bumps, think of your head and body as the car body, your feet as the wheels and your legs as the shock absorbers. Try traversing quite quickly over a line of bumps and you will get the feeling of what I mean.

You will also notice that when your feet are on the top of a bump, the tips and tails of your skis are in mid air. This is the secret to skiing bumps the easy way, using the top of the bump as a pivot point. Try it quite slowly at first. As you approach the bump, start bringing your ski sticks forward. Allow your legs to fold or be compressed by the shape of the bump as you ski on to it. Aim to plant your ski stick just on the peak. You should now be able to turn your feet and therefore your skis very easily. Extend your legs as you ski down the far side of the bump to maintain snow contact and continue turning your feet to finish the turn. Exactly the same principle applies when you ski faster, except that you will have to look further ahead to plan your route and your legs (shock absorbers) will have to move much quicker. A tip when skiing bumps fast is to aim to plant your stick just below the crest, on the near side to you, just in case you miss the top, which can be disastrous.

The secret of mogul skiing is to use the top of the bump as a pivot.

Another way to ski a mogul field is to stay in the gullies. If you were to see water running down a mogul field, it would flow through the troughs being deflected off the sides of the bumps. Skiers can do the same. It is usually a faster route down the hill and is definitely for the aggressive skier only. A tip here is to keep your legs apart a little to allow independent leg action, since one leg may be in the bottom of the trough and the other part way up the side of a bump. Plan your route further ahead than for skiing the peaks. Aim to plant your stick just below the top on the side of a bump, allowing the bump to deflect you. Try to minimize the shock of deflection by absorbing it with your legs. Remember, you will be skiing fast so it may be quite fierce. Extend your legs into the trough again and aim for the side of the next bump.

Because of the independent leg action, you should sometimes feel a pedalling effect with your feet. Skiing moguls is a lot of fun if you approach them in the right frame of mind. Don't worry about how you appear to others. Don't try to be stylish. Maintain a relatively quiet upper body, let your legs do the work and occasionally when the right bump or ridge comes along, brace your legs as you hit it and allow it to throw you into the air.

Skiing the gullies is for the very aggressive. One leg may be in the trough, another half way up a bump. Think pedalling. Look well ahead and plan your route. Aim to plant your stick below the top of the bump.

Off-piste skiing

One of the big attractions to expert skiers is 'off-piste' skiing. There are special firms of tour operators who offer specialized tours such as the 'Nine Valleys' or 'Twelve Valleys' in France. Others offer high level mountain routes such as the 'Haute Route'. In all of these cases it is *essential* to put yourself in the hands of a qualified guide. These routes can be extremely dangerous and mustn't be attempted without proper organization. Even recognizing the off-piste possibilities in your ski resort can

be tricky. In certain countries you can be held responsible if you trigger off an avalanche. You may not only be charged the cost of any rescue operation, but fined and perhaps imprisoned into the bargain. In the USA and Canada, you must obey all signs in this area of skiing. However, having said all that, there will be occasions when you will find yourself in a legitimate off-piste situation. Before you start to tackle this type of skiing, it may be as well to understand how snow is formed.

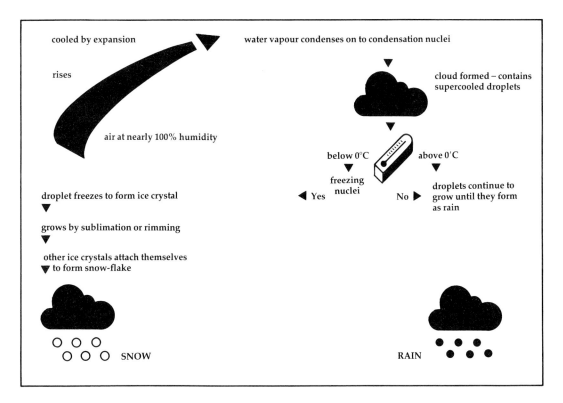

cooled by expansion

water vapour condenses on to condensation nuclei

rises

cloud formed – contains supercooled droplets

air at nearly 100% humidity

below 0°C   above 0'C

freezing nuclei

droplet freezes to form ice crystal

◀ Yes   No ▶   droplets continue to grow until they form as rain

grows by sublimation or rimming

other ice crystals attach themselves to form snow-flake

SNOW

RAIN

Ideally your turns should leave your signature in smooth, flowing arcs rather than bent straight lines.

The best way to tackle powder snow skiing is to commit yourself to the fall-line. Stand with your weight equally distributed over both feet and in the middle of the ski or just slightly back. It is something of a fallacy that in order to ski deep snow you must lean right back. It is not the case. Remember, the tips of your skis are soft and will naturally bend upward as the snow distorts them. The soft snow will slow you down somewhat and the deeper the snow, the slower you will go, so you must build up some speed before you start turning. Start to establish a rhythm by bending and stretching your legs. Exaggerate the up and down movement by

increasing the range of flex in your legs. Up to the fall-line, down out of the fall-line. As you start to turn, maintain your rhythm and relax. After a few more turns, breathe out and relax some more because you won't be as relaxed as you thought you were. At this point you may have the feeling that you are going a trifle faster than you would care to be. Don't worry, this is normal. Divert your mind to the exhilarating sensation of 'floating' instead. You are in the supreme environment for getting the most out of your ability as an expert skier. If the snow is really deep, you may have to follow the turn around with your hips and shoulders a little. In other words, rotate ever so slightly to help finish the turn.

For heavy or crusty snow, it may be easier to use the technique you used for bumps. Bend your legs by pulling your feet up underneath your body to turn to the fall-line and extend your legs out of the fall-line, continuing to turn them as you do so.

Whatever technique you use, stop at the bottom of the slope and study your tracks (sometimes referred to as 'the skier's signature'). Ideally, your turns should be linked in smooth, flowing arcs rather than bent straight lines, with a relatively narrow track. What you want to see then is a flowing signature of which you are proud.

If you are going to do lots of off-piste skiing, I suggest you invest in a pair of soft, flexible skis which are not too long.

Weight must be slightly back, but you must not lean right back.

Soft snow slows you, so speed must be built up before you start to turn. Don't panic. Enjoy the exhilaration.

Trouble shooting

SNOWPLOUGH GLIDE AND BRAKE

PROBLEM Tips splitting or crossing.
Cause Weight too far back.
Cure Bend your ankles.

PROBLEM Plough one-sided.
Cause Too much weight on one ski causing you to push out to one side only.
Cure Distribute weight evenly over both feet.

SNOWPLOUGH TURNS

PROBLEM Tips crossing.
Cause Too much rotation of hips and/or shoulders.
Cure More knee steering, less hip and shoulder movement.

TRAVERSE

PROBLEM Too much skidding of lower ski or both.
Cause Not enough edge set.
Cure Press knees and hips into the hill, turn upper body slightly downhill and lean over lower ski.
Remember – more weight on lower ski than on upper.

FINISHING TURNS – BASIC SWING ONWARD

PROBLEM Overturning and losing fluency.
Cause Too much hip and/or shoulder rotation.
Cure Practise swings to the hill, steering only with knees. Try sticks across hips again. Set sticks or slalom poles in a curve and try to follow arc.
PROBLEM Tips crossing.
Cause Too much hip rotation causing lower ski to go in front of upper, allowing upper tip to slip over lower.

Cure As above. Remember, upper ski ahead.
PROBLEM Lower tail breaking away.
Cause Too much weight on upper ski and too much hip rotation.
Cure As above. Practise also lifting tail of uphill ski and hold it there while making swing to hill.
PROBLEM Lower tip drifting away.
Cause Not enough weight on lower ski.
Cure Practise swing to hill, lifting tail of uphill ski.

UNHAPPY ON ICE

PROBLEM   Poor edge control.
Cause   Not enough weight on outside ski of turn.

Cure   Short rhythmic turns, lifting tail of inside ski with each turn. Also check that edges are sharp.

UNABLE TO CARVE A TURN ON THE STEEP

PROBLEM   Leg movements not dynamic enough.
Cause   Inexperience, weak legs, poor timing.
Cure   Miles under the skis, fitness training off skis. Practise early edge change while skiing fast.
Note: Very few skiers can make a proper carved turn.

UNHAPPY IN MOGULS

PROBLEM   Cannot hold the line (eventually moguls get you).
Cause   Bad judgement of line through moguls, legs not flexible enough, 'psyched out'.
Cure   Follow a good skier who can pick a line. Practise traversing over moguls to develop leg flexibility. Ski moguls in short sections (six or seven bumps to start with), gradually increasing length of each section.

UNHAPPY IN POWDER

PROBLEM   Uneasy because you cannot see skis. Keep falling.
Cause   Probably lack of experience and also psychological.

Cure   Experience, commitment to fall-line. Trust your skis, build up rhythm, and remember you are less likely to hurt yourself falling in powder than on piste.

SKIDDING

PROBLEM   Poor edge control.
Cause   Incorrect posture.
Cure   Hips and shoulders facing slightly downhill. Body well over feet. Practise turning feet from skidding position to traverse position back to skidding position, keeping hips and shoulders relatively still.

A tip is to fix sticks across hips by using loops. This will make you aware of how much hip movement you are making. Practise also skidding and gently lifting tail of uphill ski, holding it in the air for two or three seconds.

You're less likely to hurt yourself falling in powder . . . The 'Champagne Powder' of Park City, Utah.

Doug Lewis of the United States, racing at Aspen, demonstrates a downhiller's banking turn.

JOHN SHEDDEN AND MARTIN BELL

Part Three: Competitive skiing

Television has created a vast audience for ski racing worldwide. Downhill, because of its speed and risk, is probably the major spectacle, but the first World Championships in freestyle also attracted a big audience in 1986.

The World Cup, started in 1967, is the prime Alpine series. It covers three continents with results linked so as to provide a World Cup winner in men's and women's in the four disciplines of downhill, special slalom, giant slalom and super giant slalom. It also creates an overall winner season by season. Some of the great champions have been Karl Schranz (Austria), Jean-Claude Killy (France), Gustavo Thoeni (Italy), Ingemar Stenmark (Sweden), Franz Klammer (Austria), Phil Mahre (USA) and Marc Girardelli, Austrian born but skiing for Luxembourg. Among the outstanding women are Nancy Greene (Canada), Christine and Marielle Goitschel (France), Annemarie Moser-Proell (Austria), Rosi Mittermaier (West Germany), and Erika Hess, Maria Walliser and Michaela Figini (Switzerland).

Winter Olympics, held every four years, provide a major focal point, as do World Championships held in odd years between Olympics.

Alpine racing **MARTIN BELL**

SLALOM

Rok Petrovic of Yugoslavia, 1986 World Cup Special slalom champion, negotiates a verticale – a set of gates down the fall-line.

Format

Although slalom produces the slowest average speed of the Alpine disciplines, the racer needs more quickness of movement in this than in any other discipline. A typical slalom run lasts between 40 and 60 seconds, with between 50 and 70 gates in a course, which usually means a frequency of more than one turn per second. A gate consists of two slalom poles, alternately red and blue, of which there are two basic configurations: open gates, where the poles are set horizontally across the slope, and closed, or vertical gates, where the poles are set one below the other. A sequence of vertical gates set in a straight line down the slope (a 'verticale'), requires that the racer turn much less across the fall-line but in a quicker rhythm. There are other, more complicated gate combinations, but these occur less and less nowadays, as the modern aim in course-setting is not to catch the racer out, but to find the fastest and most consistent skier on a straightforward course.

Technique

The very short radius of slalom turns makes it impossible to carve the entire turn, so the turn can only be initiated by swivelling the skis while they are flat on the snow. The skis must be entirely weightless while this takes place but should remain in contact with the snow. As the racer approaches the slalom pole, his skis should be swivelled enough to be pointing past the pole, almost towards the next gate, and the remainder of the turn can be carved by applying maximum pressure to the ski, causing reverse camber.

At this point, it is important that the racer is in a good technical position, with extreme knee and hip angulation, and the upper body facing down the fall-line. Once past the pole, the potential energy stored in the ski can be released, causing the skier to become once more weightless. With a little practice, any excess upward momentum can be prevented from throwing the racer into the air by converting it into forward momentum, either by jetting the feet forward and bending the knees to absorb the upward kick, especially useful in deep soft snow ruts, which have a tendency to catapult a racer into the air and out of the course, or by using a scissor step. The step has an added advantage in that the outside ski does not have to be turned through as acute an angle, for part of the change in direction is achieved at the end of the turn by a step from the outside to the inside ski. The next turn can then be initiated with a pole plant.

Tamara McKinney, US World Cup title winner, adapts her native talent to the course setter's demands at Park City, Utah.

Innovations

Slalom technique has remained the same over the years, but the line taken by the racers has greatly changed since 1982, when hinged 'rapid' slalom poles were introduced. The hinge is a universal joint at snow level, connecting the base of the pole, under the snow, with the pole itself. The pole bends down easily when the racer hits it, allowing him to get much closer to the pole with his skis. He can hit the pole with his knees or even his shins (shinning the gates). Some racers had used shinning previously, but the jolt caused by a solid plastic or bamboo pole often threw the racer out of rhythm, and the pole was likely to fly out and impede the racer.

When rapid gates were first used, special padded gauntlets were introduced to punch the poles out of the way with the inside arm. Recently, lightweight slalom helmets with a peak extruding above the face and goggles, designed to take the

Yugoslavia's Bojan Krizaj on the way to a World Cup slalom victory in 1985 – wearing one of the brand-new helmets.

impact of a slalom poles, have made it much safer to shin gates. The racer no longer has to bring his inside arm into an awkward position to punch the pole, but can shin it, keeping his arms in a comfortable, wide position with better balance. Ingemar Stenmark, one of the top slalom racers for the last twelve years, began a general alteration of posture to suit the rapid gates. With solid bamboo poles, racers had to use excessive hip angulation and forward hunching of the shoulders in order to get their upper body around the pole, whereas now a more economical, upright upper body is possible as the pole has already been knocked away by the hand or shins. One drawback of this technical development is a tendency for the racer to be tempted into leaning into the gate. The Mahre twins, Phil and Steve, adhered strongly to this opinion and often trained with bamboo poles to encourage angulation. As a result, they never really adapted their style to rapid gates.

Ingemar Stenmark, the world's top slalomer for over a decade, was the first to use gauntlets for punching the hinged gates poles introduced in 1982.

Competitive skiing

Bojan Krizaj is another veteran who has adapted cleverly to new slalom demands. In this sequence shot at Kitzbuehel the Yugoslav demonstrates his marvellous flexibility.

1: At the apex of his turn Krizaj knocks down a 'rapid' pole. Extreme angulation of knee and hip give a sharp edging angle and maximum pressure over the middle of his outside ski.

2: The released pressure jets him forward weightless and airborne. His only contact with the snow is through his left pole plant.

3: The rotational impulse given by the pole plant enables him to swivel legs and skis beneath him while keeping his upper body facing down the fall line. His inside ski is slightly lifted, to avoid catching a tip on the slalom pole and to keep his weight on the outside ski.

4: By applying hard pressure to his outside ski in the previous turn he 'lands' fiercely, carving the last part of the new turn with reverse camber to the outside ski. His skis are already pointed towards the next gate, and he is poised to knock away the approaching slalom gate with his inside arm.

GIANT SLALOM

Format

This is the most physically demanding of the disciplines, each of the two runs lasting between 1 minute 10 seconds and 1 minute 30 seconds. The speeds are higher and the gates are further apart than in slalom, but there are fewer complicated gate combinations.

Technique

Giant slalom is in a way more technically difficult than slalom, as a greater part of the turn is achieved through carving and less through swivelling of the ski. The pressure is applied more gradually than in slalom, as abrupt pressure will cause the ski to break away and skid, although too

Pirmin Zurbriggen, Switzerland's giant slalom ace, using a scissor step.

1: Ingemar Stenmark is at the point of maximum pressure, approaching the gate with extreme knee and hip angulation. He is in his lowest position, with his outside leg bent, but at not too acute an angle as this would expend excess energy; from here he must extend his leg to produce acceleration.

2: He is now beginning to transfer weight to his inside ski, using a scissor step, but is finding it difficult as his outside ski is skidding and does not offer a stable platform from which to step off.

4: Stenmark is now almost weightless and allows his right ski to drift into the fall-line by swivelling his knees away from the hill and into a more neutral, unangulated position. His pole-plant also gives him the impetus to swivel to the left.

5: There is now once more pressure on Stenmark's skis, so he must angulate with his knees to make the skis carve.

3: *The outside ski is now carving cleanly. By extending his outer leg he has gained acceleration and reduced the pressure on his outer ski, stopping the skid. He is already transferring weight to his inside ski, gaining him height and a good line into the next gate.*

6: *By sinking his body position, Stenmark is gradually increasing the pressure through the turn up to a maximum just before the gate, from where he will once more extend to accelerate.*

little pressure will fail to achieve reverse camber of the ski, giving it a tendency to track straight ahead instead of carving. In giant slalom, acceleration towards the end of the turn is more important than in slalom, as the distance covered between the gates are greater. This is normally done by a scissor step from the outside to the inside ski towards the end of the turn, accompanied by an explosive upward movement to unweight the ski. As in slalom, the racer tries to shift his weight as far back as possible towards the tail of the ski at the end of the turn while still getting back over the middle of the ski for the initiation of the next turn.

Innovations

There have been few developments in giant slalom technique over the past ten years, illustrated by a comparison between photographs taken of Ingemar Stenmark and Gustavo Thoeni in 1976 and 1977, and the recent sequence of Stenmark, particularly Frame 3.

A tendency over the years to set tighter giant slaloms has often benefited slalom specialists. In the 1982 World Championships Steve Mahre, who had been very successful in slalom, but unlike his twin Phil had never won a giant slalom, gained victory on a tight, steep and icy course, in spite of wearing a knee brace on his right knee due to a recent injury. The days when downhill specialists were able to get good results in fast giant slaloms are over. The International Ski Federation (FIS) believed that there was a demand for faster giant slaloms with technical turns and gliding sections to test giant slalom and downhill specialists on an equal basis. This led in 1982 to the creation of a new discipline, Super G.

Ingemar Stenmark racing to victory in the World Cup giant slalom at Madonna di Campiglio, 1977.

SUPER G

Format

Although consisting of only one run, a Super G race is also a physically demanding competition, as a run can last between 1 minute 30 seconds and 2 minutes. Because of the average speeds of 40 to 50 miles per hour (65 to 80 kilometres per hour), all racers must wear helmets. As it is such a new discipline, World Cup Super Gs held in the last few years have varied greatly, partly due to some doubt as to what constitutes good terrain for Super G. If the terrain has a long steep section, as was the case, for example, at Puy St Vincent, then sharp turns must be set across the fall-line to control the racers' speed, which favours giant slalom specialists. Alternatively, if the terrain contains a long flat section, as in Madonna di Campiglio, much depends on gliding, an ability to keep the skis as flat as possible and to retain a low, aerodynamic body position, generally attributes of a downhill specialist. The ideal Super G terrain consists of short steep sections to gain speed through technical turns, followed by short flat sections to test gliding ability; excellent Super G races were held this year at Crans Montana and Whistler Mountain on exactly that type of terrain.

Technique

In the tighter, more technical Super Gs, you will often see the anomaly of a racer wearing a downhill-style helmet but using a giant slalom technique. In general, the pressure is kept on the outside ski for longer and less use is made of the scissor step to gain acceleration. There is more time to initiate the turn smoothly, as there is more time at the beginning of the turn. The

Martin Bell in Super G. Hands low as in downhill, but turns may be tighter.

aerodynamic tuck position is not that important at speeds of 40 miles per hour (65 kph), although giant slalom specialists are sometimes unwisely tempted to tuck as often as possible, sacrificing balance in what is, for them, a high speed event.

Luxembourg's Marc Girardelli wins the super giant slalom on the Kandahar course at Garmisch, 1985.

DOWNHILL

Format

Downhill is the fastest discipline in Alpine ski racing, with average speeds of 60 to 70 miles per hour (100–120 kph) and top speeds of 80 to 90 miles per hour (130–150 kph). This is still slower than the sport of speed-skiing, where the racers attain over 120 miles per hour (190 kph) on a straight track, but downhill differs from this in that there are turns, jumps and compressions to be negotiated at high speed. Paradoxically, the most selective

Below: At the point of take-off, Martin Bell is pushing his hands forward to achieve forward rotation and pulling his knees to his chest to 'suck' the jump

Below right: In the air, he attempts to hold as tight a position as possible.
Below: The legs are slightly extended before the landing to absorb the impact and the sticks are already under the arms in order to adopt the tuck position immediately after regaining contact with the snow.

parts of the course are often the slower sections, consisting of tight turns where the racer's speed can drop from 80 to 50 miles per hour (130 to 80 kph) in a matter of seconds. The racer who loses the least momentum through a tight turn will be the one with the best technique, and slalom specialists can often compete on equal terms with the downhill specialists through such a section of the course.

Unlike the other Alpine disciplines, racers are allowed to practise on the downhill course for two to three days before the event. This practice is organized in the form of two to five official timed training runs, of which a racer must start at least one. If a downhiller is on a course which is new to him, he will take it easy for the first couple of training runs, taking a high line into the turns to give himself more room, and standing up before the bigger jumps, to slow himself down in order not to fly as far. In the classic races, where the courses do not vary much from year to year, an experienced downhiller has a great advantage, as he can go at full speed in the first training runs and build up his confidence with good training times.

Training runs can also be used to test equipment, primarily skis. On a flat, straight section, gliding ability is essential, but will be of no help if the racer's skis are slow, for a pair of slow skis can mean a deficit of two to four seconds over a full-length course. Waxing is less important than the actual choice of skis, as no amount of fast wax can make a slow pair of skis go fast. To ensure that their racers get the best material, the ski manufacturers test hundreds of pairs of downhill skis through the autumn and give the fastest

ones to their established stars for the first races of the winter, making it more difficult for young racers to make a breakthrough.

Technique

Downhill technique requires a similar stance in the turns to the other disciplines, but it is possible for a racer to get away with less hip angulation, and the upper body should be more bent to reduce wind drag. A turn should be started very gradually by rolling the knee over to put the ski on edge without swivelling. It is easier to maintain pressure on the outside ski throughout the turn as the centrifugal force is greater than in the other disciplines. Downhill skis are longer, at 223 cms, and stiffer than recreational skis, but they still function due to reverse camber.

Martin Bell in downhill. Here the reverse camber of the ski is clearly visible.

Whenever the downhiller is not turning, he will be trying to hold his tuck position. This must be the most aerodynamic, but also the most comfortable position to suit his individual build. In the conventional tuck, the arms are in front of the body, as this is better for balance. The poles are bent, not to improve their own aerodynamic properties, but to make it more comfortable for the racer to tuck his elbows in front of his knees. Some racers hold their hands up in front of their chins, whereas others feel they have better balance with their hands lower and further forward.

A compression is a concave feature of a downhill course where three or four times the racer's body weight pushes down upon him, very much as if he were at the bottom of a roller-coaster. It is essential to a racer's survival that he keep his centre of gravity well forward, or else he will be

Champion stuff: No downhiller stays in his tuck over bumps better than Switzerland's Karl Alpiger.

pushed back until he is sitting on the tails of his skis; then it is only a matter of time until disaster occurs.

The same principle applies to jumps. A downhiller is thrown into the air as the ground beneath him changes from flat to steep. He must push his weight forward as he goes over the lip, so that the angle of his body corresponds to the new gradient of his landing area. If his weight is too far back, the wind will catch under the tips of his skis and flip him on to his back, the most common type of fall amongst down-hillers. When a downhiller is seen wind-milling with his arms in mid-air, it is not in itself a fault but merely the body's instinc-tive reaction to correct a mistake which has already been made at take-off. There is also a need to absorb the upward kick imparted to the racer by the lip of the jump. Originally, this was done by pre-jumping, where the racer jumps away of his own accord before the lip of the jump, hopefully landing just on the far side. This

World Cup titleholder Marc Girardelli flails to retain balance on the Aspen downhill course.

technique is now rarely used at high speed; if the racer pre-jumps too early, he could land on top of the lip and take off again, usually out of control; if he pre-jumps too late, he will practically be launching himself off the jump. A more reliable technique is to 'suck' the jump, bending the knees and pushing the hands forward. In general, more time is lost or gained in turns than on jumps, but the key to jumping is survival; Peter Mueller lost the 1986 Downhill World Cup by twice crashing on jumps, at a time when he was skiing the turns well enough to win the race. On the other hand, Bill Johnson won the 1984 Olympics on a Sarajevo course that contained many jumps but not many difficult turns, by maintaining an aerodynamic position in the air.

Downhill is not regarded as a technical discipline, as it allows more freedom for individual skiing ability. Although there is an ideal line, it is still possible to win a race after deviating from that line, even by

Peter Mueller is not as low in the tuck as some but he has a fine feeling for his skis.

The downhill course at Kitzbuehel: the finish, January 1984.

several metres, which is not possible in the technical disciplines. Peter Mueller is regarded by many as having less than perfect technique, but he compensates by a very fine feeling for his skis.

Innovation

Since downhill suit fabrics were standardized by the FIS in the seventies, there have been few developments to improve aerodynamic properties. Four years ago, a helmet manufacturer decided to give the helmets a matt finish, in order to cut down turbulence, but in practice it did not seem to make much difference. New tuck positions have been experimented with, but they are all inferior to the conventional position in terms of balance and stability, even if they may be fractionally faster.

SPECIALIZATION

Normally, racers are able to reach world class standard in, at most, two of the four disciplines mentioned in this chapter. In spite of the fact that the FIS have built into the World Cup formula many incentives for racers to excel at all four disciplines, the number of racers who have achieved this can be counted on the fingers of one hand. This is partly due to the race schedule, which requires racers to make very gruelling journeys to get from one race to the other, if they are trying to race in all four disciplines. Given the amount of time needed to train for even one event, the only way for any but the most naturally talented racers to make it to the top will be by specialization.

Peter Mueller reveals the grim determination that is necessary to reach world class standard.

Freestyle

JOHN SHEDDEN

The sport of Freestyle emerged out of American 'hot dog skiing' and became accepted by the FIS in 1981. It is a demonstration sport at the Olympic Games in Calgary in 1988.

Freestyle is particularly attractive to many British skiers because training for it can begin on dry slopes, trampolines and water ramps and continue to very high levels of skill, without the need to use large tracts of mountainside as in downhill racing. Its origins in North America also mean that the language and much of the literature of Freestyle is in English; and being a sport which encourages self-expression it has found favour with Britain's youth.

Aspen staged the first freestyle in 1971. Tignes hosted the first World Championships in 1986. At Calgary in 1988 it is a Winter Olympics demonstration event. Here, Donald Gordon demonstrates Aerial acrobatics. Judges award marks for quality of take-off, height and distance.

THE FREESTYLE DISCIPLINES

Aerials

Aerial acrobatics on skis is the most spectacular, yet in some ways the most controversial discipline.

The competition consists of two different acrobatic leaps, taken individually from a prepared jump or ramp, specifically designed for either upright jumps, forward or backward somersaults. The take-off and landing are performed on skis, but otherwise no skiing skill is required.

In training, gymnastic and trampolining abilities are developed to the full, but skis must be used to gain marks, and so water ramps provide this refinement to basic training.

In competitions the judges award marks for quality of take-off, height and distance. This is known as *air*.

The most dangerous part of this manoeuvre is obviously the *landing* and so the judges require that 'the competitor should demonstrate a balanced, stable position throughout, with precision, grace and good absorption with the legs'. Marks may be deducted if a competitor falls.

The majority of the marks are given for the *form* in the air. Timing, precision and body shapes are all evaluated while the competitor may, in top competitions, be making several full twists of the body whilst completing up to three somersaults.

The marks gained from air (20 per cent maximum), landing (30 per cent maximum) and form (50 per cent maximum) are then multiplied by a degree of difficulty factor to obtain the performance score.

Britain's Mike Nemesvary achieved world class before a trampoline accident left him paralysed.

As a form of training, aerial competitions are held on water ramps where skiers land in the water. Aerial competitions have been excluded from all competitions held on dry ski slopes because of the potential injury hazard and possible long term effects on the skier's hips and spine.

Moguls

Competitors compete against the clock within a free run of a mogul field and achieve points (25 per cent maximum) in relation to their *time*.

Aerial manoeuvres are also included and marks up to (25 per cent maximum) are given for height, spontaneity, controlled landing and resumption of rhythm which should deviate as little as possible from the fall-line. Most points are however awarded by the judges (50 per cent maximum) for the quality and technical evaluation of the skiers.

Use of rather than avoidance of the moguls is marked highly and absorption of the bumps should be made with the whole legs, using only bending from the waist in extreme circumstances. Rhythm and positive attack are favoured highly as well.

These events are usually run on parallel courses with a divider down the middle of the mogul field. The winner of each heat goes through to the next round. I suspect that the complexity of scoring this discipline makes the judges' task as hard as the competitors'.

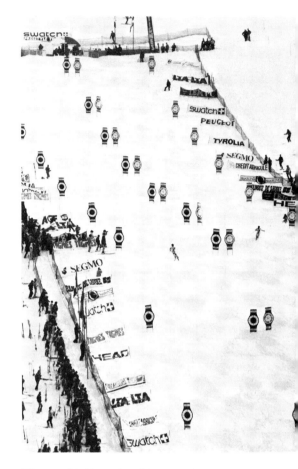

The World Championship Moguls course at Tignes in France, 1986. Judges award marks according to style and technical competence over a steepish field of bumps.

Ballet

Ballet skiing may be done on shorter than normal skis, according to a length of ski table and using longer than normal ski sticks, but never longer than head height. One descent on a smoothly prepared piste is judged against criteria of fluency, grace and complexity of manoeuvres which includes jumps, spins, somersaults and various steps linked together in harmony with the skier's own choice of music.

In assessing the descent, the judges consider the sequence and the utilization of space. The skier's personal carriage or posture is marked highly along with ease and flow of movements in a programme which also shows virtuosity.

In training, the use of ballet dance and ice skating practices are utilized. The choreography is a major element of the final production, as is the choice of music. All these factors are secondary however to the skier's own ability to feel for the flow of movements from foot to foot – forwards and backwards, to be sensitive in balancing within dance forms on a sliding edge and to improvise where errors of timing are made.

Julia Snell demonstrates ski ballet, the third element of Freestyle. Jumps, spins, somersaults and various steps are linked to the accompaniment of music chosen by the competitor.

The Cairngorns on a fine day.

Glossary

F – French.   G – German.   I – Italian.

Abfahrt (G) Downhill ski run. (F. Descente.) A test of speed and courage over two or three miles for men and one to one and a half miles for women.

Abonnement (F) Season ticket for lifts and lessons.

Achtung! (G) Danger! Look out! (F. Piste! I. Pista!)

Aerials Freestyle discipline involving acrobatic jumps.

Alm Mountain pasture.

Alpine racing Downhill, super giant slalom, giant slalom and slalom races.

Anti-friction pad Slipper pad behind toe piece of binding to ensure prompt release of boot.

Artificial slope Practice slope made of plastic bristle.

Ausgang (G) Way out.

Avalement (F) Technique at the start and finish of fast turns requiring quick, flexible knee bends with feet thrust forward. Also: Jet.

Bahnhof (G) Station.

Ballet Freestyle discipline using ballet-style movements.

BASI British Association of Ski Instructors.

Basket Disc near base of ski pole to limit penetration into snow.

Biathlon Competition which combines cross-country skiing with target shooting.

Bindings Devices which attach boot to ski.

Birdsnesting Choosing to ski off-piste among trees.

Black run A difficult, steep marked run for advanced skiers.

Bloodwagon Sledge to transport injured skiers from the mountain.

Blue run Marked run for intermediate skiers.

Brake Spring-loaded prong attached to binding which stop skis from sliding away after a fall on piste.

Breakable crust Hard-surface snow, soft underneath.

Bubble Gondola-style lift.

Bucket Basic, cage-like lift with no seats.

Bum-bag Small pack attached to belt around waist.

Button One-person drag lift with supporting disc instead of bar.

Cable car Large cabin lift with no seats suspended from overhead lines. (G. Luftseilbahn. F. Téléphérique.)

Camber Arched shape of ski when no weight is applied.

Carved turn Turn in which ski moves in its own track with minimal skidding.

Chair lift Overhead suspension transport usually with open seat. (G. Sesselbahn. F. Télésiège. I. Seggiovia.)

Chill factor Drop in temperature due to cooling effect of wind.

Christiania Family of turns down and across the fall-line. Usually abbreviated to christie. Parallel christie: skis together. Stem christie: outside ski fans out in a skidding motion, returning to parallel in traverse.

Circus Series of linking lifts and runs which allow small tours.

Compact ski Short ski (about head height) easy to manoeuvre.

Compression Section of downhill course where ground flattens or rises.

Cornice Overhang of snow at top of snow caused by wind.

Couloir Steep, narrow descent.

Crevasse Crack in glacier ice, often covered by snow.

Cross-country Skiing over undulating terrain using narrow, light-weight skis attached by toe clips to soft shoe allowing heel to rise.

DIN German standards organisation for ski equipment design.

Downhill Alpine race at speed with fewer turns.

Drag lift System of cables by which skiers are pulled up the slopes, with skis sliding in tracks. T-bar style for two people. Button (Disc) for individuals.

Edging Weighting the metal edge of skis to achieve a check or turn.

Eingang (G) Way in.

Fall-line The steepest and most direct slope below a skier at any given point.

Fasching (G) Lenten carnival, celebrated especially in Austria, which generates crowds on slopes and streets and can result in higher seasonal prices.

Fermé (F) Closed. (Indicates a run that is dangerous or has poor snow.) (G. Geschlossen, Gesperrt.)

FIS Fédération Internationale de Ski. The world governing body of skiing.

Flofit Padded inner boot which adapts to the contours of the foot.

Foam injection Method of filling inner boot with foam to create a perfect individual fit.

Föhn (G) Warm wind creating thaw.

Freestyle skiing Competitive variant of Alpine skiing combining acrobatic, ballet and mogul discplines.

Funicular Tracked railway for steep slopes.

Gaiter Waterproof material, elasticated at both ends, to keep snow from penetrating top of ski boot.

Gaststube (G) Guest house. (F. Pension.)

Giant slalom One-mile Alpine race to test traversing ability through a series of well-spaced gates.

Glacier Ice mass. Summer skiing is often on glaciers.

GLM Graduated length method. American teaching system in which pupils graduate from short (1.35m) to longer lengths of ski as they progress. (F. Ski évolutif.)

Glühwein (G) Hot, spiced wine. (F. Vin chaud; I. Vino caldo.)

Gondola Cabin cableway for two or four persons. Also known as Bubbles. (F. Télécabines; G. Gondelbahn.)

Grass skiing Skiing with short caterpillar tread skis on grassy slopes.
Green run The easiest of graded ski runs.
Gunbarrel Trail with upward-sloping sides like a gutter.

Heli-skiing Skiing using helicopter transport.
Herringbone Reverse snow plough method of climbing a slope on foot.
Hockey stop Uphill christie.
Hot-dogging Mogul skiing.

Inside ski Uphill ski.

Joch (G) Pass linking two peaks.
Jump turn Parallel turn in steep or difficult conditions.

Kick turn Changing direction through 180° from a stationary position.

Langlauf (G) Touring or cross-country skiing. (Langrenn. Norwegian.) Known also as Ski du Fond (F). Cross-country skiing and jumping are collectively known as Nordic, as opposed to Alpine, skiing.
Lehrer (G) Instructor. (F. Moniteur.)
Loipe Marked trail for Nordic skiers.
Low season Periods of winter during which package holidays are cheaper, avoiding crowds at Christmas, Fasching, Easter and the traditional French ski week in February.

Moguls Bumps made by the repeated passage of skiers.
Motorway Broad, easy piste. Often featureless.

Nordic skiing Cross-country skiing and ski jumping.
Nursery slopes Gentle gradients where beginners learn the rudiments of skiing.

Off-piste Area of skiing away from marked, maintained and patrolled ski runs.
Offen (G) Open: Run open. (F. Ouvert.)
Outside ski Downhill ski.

Parablocks Plastic boxes fitted to the top of skis to help prevent them crossing in downhill racing or soft snow.
Piste (F) Marked track for Alpine skiers implicitly with harder, prepared snow and more bumps (moguls) because of the frequent passage of skiers. Also: Trail.
Pole Ski stick. (F. Bâton; G. Stock.)
Pole plant Use of the inside ski pole to initiate a turn, both timing it and helping with the up-unweighting.
Poma Button lift.
Porridge Sticky, lumpy snow.
Powder snow New, low-temperature, light-textured snow.
Principianti (I) Beginners. (F. Débutantes; G. Anfänger.)
Projection circulaire (F) Turn of the body and skis with outside arm leading.
P-Tex Ski sole material giving permanently waxed effect. Gouges can be repaired with a polythene candle.

Ratrac Snow tractor used to prepare pistes. (Also: snow cat; piste basher.)
Reverse camber Weighting of a ski so it bores into the snow.

Safety strap Strap attached to binding and clipping round the ankle to prevent the ski running away in a fall. Largely replaced by the brake.
Schuss (G) Straight run down the fall-line without checks.
Scissors turn Form of step turn.
Sidecut Narrowing, or waisting, of ski between tip and tail.

Side slip Controlled sideways slide.

Sidestepping Controlled up and down movement, on skis.

Ski stoppers U-shaped sprung clips with prongs attached to bindings which dig into the snow and prevent ski sliding away after a fall. (*See also* Brake.)

Slalom Race of about 575 metres down a one-in-three slope through approximately 75 gates of beflagged, spring-loaded poles not less than 3.2 metres apart. Test of turning ability.

Snowplough Movement down or near the fall-line with skis in a 'V' position, tips together, ski soles turning to varying degrees, literally like a plough.

Snowplough turn Change of direction made by weighting one or other of the skis when they are in the 'V' position.

Speed skiing Race on a vertical course, without turns, to achieve maximum velocity.

Steilhang (G) Especially steep slope, a feature of a classic downhill race,

Stem Outward fanning movement of one or both skis, either to start a turn (*see* Christiania) or to take up the plough position.

Step turn Parallel turn initiated by a step uphill.

Super G Alpine racing discipline, a cross between Downhill and Giant Slalom.

Swing Shallow turn.

Telemark Method of turning when skiing down a slope with cross-country skis, which cannot be 'edged' like downhill skis.

Tip Front part of ski.

Tramlines Ruts.

Traverse Movement across a slope.

Tuck Egg-like posture adopted by downhill skiers as they crouch to increase their speed.

Turntable binding Binding with rotating heel piece.

Unweighting Method whereby a skier briefly lifts his weight from the skis to assist a turn.

Verboten (G) Forbidden. (F. Défense de . . . .)

Waist Narrow part of ski.

Wall Steep, wide descent.

Wedel (G) Short, fast linked turns on flat or nearly flat skis down the fall-line. (F. Godilles.)

White-out Weather conditions which much reduce visibility.

Windslab Unstable snow caused by wind over its surface.

Addresses

British Ski Federation, 118 Eaton Square, London SW1W 9AF
Tel: 01 235 8227

English Ski Council, Area Library Building, The Precinct, Halesowen, West Midlands B63 4AJ
Tel: 021 501 2314

Scottish National Ski Council,
110a Maxwell Avenue, Bearsden, Glasgow G64 4BR
Tel: 041 943 0760

Ski Council of Wales, P O Box 3, Chepstow, Gwent NP6 6NJ
Tel: 029 12 71222

Combined Services Winter Sports Association, 4 Clive Road, Strawberry Vale, Twickenham TW1 4SG
Tel: 01 892 9900

Ulster Ski Council, 43 Ballymaconnell Road, Bangor, County Down, Northern Ireland
Tel: 0247 473134

British Association of Ski Instructors, Inverdruie Visitors Centre, Inverdruie, Aviemore, Inverness-shire PH22 1QH
Tel: 0479 810407

British Alpine Racing Ski Clubs, Manor Farm, Astwood Bank, Redditch, Worcs.

Ski Club of Great Britain, 118 Eaton Square, London SW1W 9AF
Tel: 01 245 1033

The British Ski Slope Operators Association, Ski Rossendale, Haslingden Old Road, Rawtenstall, Rossendale BB4 8RR
Tel: 0706 228844

Association of British Ski Operators, 118 Eaton Square, London SW1W 9AF
Tel: 01 235 8227

Skiing Conditions in Scotland (recorded message) Tel: 031 246 8031

Australia Australian Ski Federation, Olympia Park, Swan Street, Melbourne, 3002 Victoria
Tel: (03) 429 8066

Austria Österreichischer Skiverband, Olympia Strasse, 10 A-6020, Innsbruck
Tel: (05) 222 221 43

Canada Canadian Ski Association, 333 River Road Tower A, Vanier, Ontario K1L 8HP
Tel: 613 748 5660

France Fédération Française de Ski, 50 rue des Marquisats, B.P. 451, F-74009, Annecy
Tel 50 51 40 34

Switzerland Fédération Suisse de Ski, Schosshaldens Strasse, 32 Postfach ch-3000, Berne 32
Tel: (031) 434 444

Acknowledgements

The demonstrators used in this book are members of the demonstration team of The British Association of Ski Instructors (BASI).

Apart from being the recognized body for the training and grading of ski instructors in Britain, BASI are also members of the International Ski Instructors Association (ISIA). Every four years, the member nations of the ISIA get together in some part of the world and hold an International Ski Instructors Congress (Interski), to exchange information and ideas on the developments of skiing and ski techniques. Many of the countries use a demonstration team to illustrate their techniques. These skiers are among the best in their own countries and indeed the world.

Our sincere thanks to BASI for their help and advice and the services of their demonstrators, Sue Dickson and Roy Bisset.

First published 1986 by Pan Books Ltd, Cavaye Place, London SW10 9PG

9 8 7 6 5 4 3 2 1

© British Ski Federation 1986

Designer: Peter Ward
Photographs © Mark Junak 1986

Additional photo credits
George Herringshaw, Associated Sports
Photography   108
Patrick McDowell, Park City Ski Area   117
Associated Press   118, 119 (top), 121, 124, 126
Graham Watson   119 (bottom)
John Eddowes   116, 122–3, 125, 133

ISBN 0 330 29558 6 paperback

Photoset by Parker Typesetting Service, Leicester
Printed and bound in Great Britain by
R. J. Acford, Chichester, Sussex